A
COLLECTION
OF MONKEYS

Mario Kiefer

ISBN-13: 978-0692151853 (Mario Kiefer)

ISBN-10:0692151850

For Ric, always.

ABOUT THE AUTHOR

Mario Kiefer has a keen interest in people and likes to write about the things that make people tick — those hidden motivations they often do not see themselves. Although born in Austin, Texas, he has lived in many parts of the country and is fascinated by the differing cultural viewpoints he has encountered always asking himself "why"?

Other Works by this author include:
- The Ordinary Life (November 2017)
- The Ordinary Doll (Coming in the fall 2018)

George Orwell once wrote:

"If liberty means anything at all, it means the right to tell people what they do not want to hear."

March 15, 2016

It must be the political season. So much of what I see on social media seems to be political rants from both the right and the left denigrating the other side.

But nobody is 100% evil and nobody is 100% good. Each and every one of us is a flawed individual. Have we really become so jaded and so biased in our own prejudices that we cannot see any good in those with whom we disagree?

I truly hope that someday, instead of seeing the hateful and mean-spirited rhetoric that masquerades as political thought (coming from both sides of the debate), we can learn to say something positive about those with whom we disagree. I hope that on that day, I will see decent and respectful civil discourse. But alas, I fear that may never be. Please prove me wrong.

March 20, 2016

I read a post today trumpeting the efforts of those who would stop a presidential rally. I understand that there are those who do not like the speaker, but attempting to prevent someone from speaking, or trying to stop others from hearing him speak, well, that just strikes me as antithetical to American ideals. Whatever happened to freedom of speech, political thought and ideology? Are they now gone? Yes, yes, I know the First Amendment only protects our freedom of speech from governmental censorship, but still . . . do we not hold these ideals outside of government intervention?

For democracy to thrive, all voices must be heard. Silencing one voice over others does not allow each point of view to be considered. Dissent is an essential facet of a working democracy. Democracy dies, when only those with the *"right"* position are allowed to express their position. If the masses are not allowed to hear another who says something that is not considered *"right"* by one portion of society, they become frustrated and feel disenfranchised.

If we want civil unrest, then, by all means, silence the other side, but if we want a strong, vibrant democracy, we must allow each side to have their say, to speak and to be heard; to give voice to the anger and frustration that so many feel.

When so-called protesters prohibit speech, or prevent another from hearing words with which they disagree, that anger and frustration only build and fuel the fire of discord. Moreover, those who do not support the other side will move to that side, because they sense the inherent *"wrongness"* of the attempted censorship. The anger and frustration is fueled.

There is no doubt that the very thing these protestors oppose, will come to pass. When it does, they will have nobody to blame but themselves. It will occur, in large part, because of the very actions they take in trying to prevent it.

JUNE 14, 2016

There was another terrorist attack. This time, the terrorist struck a gay nightclub in Orlando, Florida.

I wonder . . .

Does anyone else find it interesting that, in one masterful stroke, the terrorist has turned our attention away from the fight against terrorism? Just as the news breaks that we are making headway in routing ISIS from Fallujah; that troops are nearing Raqqa; and that ISIS has lost so much of its territory, we are debating gun control, gay rights, homophobia, and our own intolerance — oblivious to the War on Terror.

The political left rallies toward implementation of stricter gun control laws. The political right rallies toward a ban on Muslim immigration. We segregate ourselves into our respective camps and argue with each other. We point fingers at the "*other*" side of the aisle. We call for unity, while we display appalling disunity.

And the band plays on.

June 15, 2016

I woke this morning and checked my Facebook feed:

8 posts blaming lack of gun control for the massacre in Orlando;

6 posts blaming Republicans for the massacre in Orlando;

5 posts blaming Democrats for the massacre in Orlando;

2 posts blaming homophobia for the massacre in Orlando.

The number of posts blaming the terrorist and perpetrator, Omar Mateen, for the massacre in Orlando — zero.

It seems that everyone and everything is to blame — except for the man who pulled the trigger . . . and the band plays on.

JUNE 18, 2016

In recent days, I have often seen a meme on Facebook (especially before the Republican and Democratic conventions) complaining about the electoral process and urging people to get rid of pledged/super-delegates and the electoral college, proclaiming them to be un-democratic. I believe this meme shows a fundamental misunderstanding of the American system and, further, it conflates two entirely different issues.

First, pledged/super-delegates are the construct of political parties. They are used by some political parties to select the party's candidate for president. A party's nominating process is (and should be) entirely at the discretion of that party's members. In point of fact, not every political party has conventions, nor does each use pledged or super-delegates.

There is no Constitutional requirement that a political party do anything at all in its selection process. Each political party must determine their own process. If a political party chooses its candidate for president by a potato sack race — it is free to do so. If a member of that

5

party prefers a different method of choosing its nominee, he may work within the rules of his party to affect change to that method or if he cannot affect such change, and still finds the manner by which the party makes its choice objectionable, he is free to leave that party to join another whose nomination process is more in line with his way of thinking. Calls to rid the process of superdelegates on a national scale are misplaced. The determination of what is appropriate for the party is at the discretion of the party.

Second, as to the Electoral College: When we call for the direct election of the President, we forget the purpose of the Electoral College. The United States was initially organized under the Articles of Confederation as a federation of sovereign states under the umbrella of a federal system of government. The purpose of that federal government was to coordinate the common interests of the many states.

After our founding, it was a dozen years, or so, later when we adopted our Constitution. That document was meant to guarantee the rights of individual states under the aegis of the federal system, while unifying the several states in such a way that, before its implementation, was not evident under the Articles of Confederation. The Constitution, set forth the role of the federal government as one with clearly defined and certain rights and responsibilities. It proclaimed that all rights and responsibilities not specifically conferred on the federal government fell under the purview of the states. Because some states had larger populations than others, the smaller states in our confederation were concerned that their interests would not be met by direct election of a President. The compromise was the Electoral College which was designed to ensure that these smaller states would not have to capitulate to the desires of larger states with greater populations. Not having direct election of the US executive was a specific design to protect the rights of the minority from the tyranny of the majority. Calls to change this system are misplaced in that those calls remove those protections.

Third, members of Congress are elected by each of the several states to represent the people of their state in that federal system. (Initially, senators were appointed by the states, but that changed under the 17th Amendment to the Constitution.) The role of each legislator within Congress is to represent the interests of his or her state — not the interest of a political party. Representatives from California, for example, are meant to represent the will of Californians; Texas representatives, of Texans, etc. We do not elect Republicans or Democrats to represent a party platform, but increasingly, it seems our legislators have forgotten that simple truth and are more interested in party politics than in representing their respective constituencies.

The government of the United States is organized under a *federal* system — not a national government. It was not until the 1900s that we began to grow the role of the federal government in such a way that we now ask that government to act as if it were, in fact, a national government. Because, it was not designed to be such, increasingly it fails in its attempts.

If we want to change our system to one that is in accord with a national system, then we must change our Constitution to reflect that desire. If we want to maintain the federal system that was designed by our forefathers, then we must reign the federal government back within its proper role. A federal government cannot succeed in what we ask it to do if we ask it to act as if it were a national government. It simply does not have the appropriate structure to succeed in that role.

JUNE 23, 2016

To my Republican Friends:

Please do not say that you are tolerant of everyone, then demonize those with whom you disagree.

Please do not say that you believe in diversity, then demonize minorities and other religions.

Please do not say that you are pro-life, then support the death penalty.

Please do not say that you are for individual liberty, but then regulate what one does with another consenting adult.

Be consistent in your beliefs.

To my Democratic Friends:

Please do not say that you are tolerant of everyone, then demonize those with whom you disagree.

Please do not say that you believe in diversity, then demonize white, heterosexual males and Christians.

Please do not say that you are pro-choice, then attempt to restrict one's access to tobacco, sugary drinks or other foods.

Be consistent in your beliefs.

To each and all: Do not be hypocrites.

June 26, 2016

When we are very young, we look to our parents for guidance.

When we become a teenager, nothing our parents tell us is right.

When we are in college, everything our parents say is old fashioned and out-of-touch.

In our thirties, we turn to our parents for guidance.

And then we miss them when they are gone.

Mario Kiefer

June 26, 2016

"*When in the Course of human events, it becomes necessary for one people to dissolve the political bands which have connected them with another, and to assume among the powers of the earth, the separate and equal station to which the Laws of Nature and of Nature's God entitle them, a decent respect to the opinions of mankind requires that they should declare the causes which impel them to the separation.*

"*We hold these truths to be self-evident, that all men are created equal, that they are endowed by their Creator with certain unalienable Rights, that among these are Life, Liberty and the pursuit of Happiness. — That to secure these rights, Governments are instituted among Men, deriving their just powers from the consent of the governed, — That whenever any Form of Government becomes destructive of these ends, it is the Right of the People to alter or to abolish it, and to institute new Government, laying its foundation on such principles and organizing its powers in such form, as to them shall seem most likely to effect their Safety and Happiness. Prudence, indeed, will dictate that Governments long established should not be changed for light and transient causes; and accordingly all experience hath shewn, that mankind are more disposed to suffer, while evils are sufferable, than to right themselves by abolishing the forms to which they are accustomed. But when a long train of abuses and usurpations, pursuing invariably the same Object evinces a design to reduce them under absolute Despotism, it is their right, it is their duty, to throw off such Government, and to provide new Guards for their future security."*

These are the words that begin the United States Declaration of Independence.

These very words proclaim that a people have the right to self-determination. Changes in the institutions of government should not be taken lightly, but that the people of a society — any society — have the right to make that determination.

In the United States today, I see much railing against the Brexit vote. I, for one, believe that is likely not a good idea. But the people of the UK have spoken in an electoral process. The people of the UK have that right to self-determination.

We should not argue against that right simply because we do not like the determination that has been set.

July 3, 2016

Feeling bewildered:

Gunmen, pledging allegiance to ISIS, attacked a nightclub in France. Scores of people were dead and/or wounded. The world mourned. Many on Facebook changed their profile pics to include pictures of the French flag with the saying, "*Je Suis Paris*" scored underneath.

A lone gunman entered a nightclub in Orlando pleading allegiance to ISIS. Scores of people were dead and/or wounded. The world mourned. Many on Facebook changed their profile pics to include pictures of a rainbow flag with the saying, "*We stand with Orlando*" scored underneath.

Gunmen, suspected to be with ISIS, attacked an airport in Turkey. Scores of people were dead and/or wounded . . . where are the Facebook posts with the Turkish flags saying, "*We stand with Turkey*"?

Gunmen, pledging allegiance to ISIS, attacked a cafe in Bangladesh. Scores of people were dead and/or wounded . . . where are the Facebook posts with the Bangladeshi flags saying, "*We stand with Bangladesh*"?

When one is wronged, do we stand with him? Or do we stand only with the aggrieved if we like him?

JULY 9, 2016

In our zeal to promote our positions on issues, we demonize the other side. We forget that mere disagreement on an issue does not equate to evil. As a society, we have forgotten how to disagree without being disagreeable. We have forgotten that words have consequences. We must learn these things anew.

Those who support one candidate for president over the other are not all (as one post called them) *"racists, bigots, misogynists, ignorant or just plain stupid."*

Those who support one candidate for president over the other are not all (as one post called them) *"naive, stupid, lying idiots."*

Not all Republicans are (as one post called them) *"fucking idiots."*

Not all Democrats are (as one post said) *"trying to destroy this nation."*

If we cannot learn to have reasoned discussion and debate about the serious issues that face our nation without resorting to *ad hominem* attacks, name calling, and generally irresponsible commentary, then we will never be able to solve our problems. If we continue down a path of demonizing anyone (and everyone) with whom we disagree, our words can, and only will, lead to violence.

When we call another *"evil,"* we are calling for violence. After all, is not it incumbent upon us destroy *"evil"*? It would behoove each and every one of us to refrain from rhetoric that leads to deeds that lead to violence that leads to death.

As a society, we must wake to the circumstances around us. As individuals, we must recognize that our own words have consequences. We must remember that whenever we speak (or publish to some social media site) our words, especially when spoken out of emotion, have consequences. We must be respectful of each other and each other's opinions, especially when we disagree.

JULY 10, 2016

Everything I need to know, I learned at the teat of my mother before I was five years old. Here are some of the things she used to say:

"Opinions are like assholes — everybody's got one. Assholes are like opinions — they aren't meant to be shared with everybody."

"Go, do it again so you learn not to."

"I love you too, or I wouldn't put up with your shit."

"Birds of a feather flock together and I don't want to hang out with the pigeons."

"A stiff cock has no morals — it will go into any hole."

"Just because you can doesn't mean that you should."

"If wishes were fishes we'd all cast nets. Careful what you wish for, you just might get it."

"Alone you can move a pile of dirt, but together we can move a mountain."

"You came into this world naked and alone. When you leave you are going to be naked and alone. How you spend your time between now and then is up to you."

"Decide what kind of man you want to be. Don't let others decide for you."

"I'm a liberal. I believe that people have the right to choose for themselves. I am also a conservative. I believe that people are responsible for their own choices and have to face the consequences for them. Make your choice, but don't bitch and moan about what happens after."

"America may be a democracy, but this is my house and my house is a dictatorship where I am the queen. If you don't like my rules, the door is that-a-way, don't let it hit you on the ass on the way out."

"Don't rely on someone else to take care of you. You are responsible for your own life."

"I don't care how big you get, I will whip your ass even if I have to stand on a chair to do it."

"Don't let emotion cloud your judgment."

"Sometimes, you are so smart that your stupid. The smartest people in the room too often have no common sense."

What I would give to have that woman's guidance once again.

JULY 12, 2016

We all remember the story . . .

There was once a boy who cried wolf. The townsfolk got up in arms and went out in search of evidence of the wolf. Finding none, they chalked it up to mistake and went about their daily chores.

The boy liked the attention, so he continued to cry wolf on many occasions. Each time, the townsfolk went off in search of the wolf, but never found hide nor hair of the creature. The boy cried wolf so often that the townsfolk began to disbelieve his cries and, after some time, they no longer responded to them.

It came to pass, that one day the boy, in fact, saw a wolf. He cried out to the townsfolk, *"There is a wolf in our midst!"* But, alas, nobody believed him. Because nobody believed him, he was eaten by the wolf.

It strikes me that so much of what we see published on social media and/or perpetuated by the broadcast or print media is like that boy who cried wolf. We re-post memes that are factually inaccurate. We denigrate or make salacious comments about individuals based on little or no evidence. We do this, and others begin to ignore these statements. They stop believing what the poster has to say.

We should each take care to not be eaten by the wolf.

Modern American Politics

DEMS: The Republican candidate is unfit for office.

REPS: The Democrat candidate is unfit for office.

DEMS: The Republican candidate is a bigot and a racist.

REPS: The Democrat candidate is crooked and a liar.

DEMS: The Republican candidate's ties are made in China

REPS: The Democrat candidate wears stupid pantsuits.

DEMS: The Republican candidate is orange from spray tanning.

REPS: The Democrat candidate is ugly and has fat hips.

DEMS: The Republican candidate is a stupid, poopeyhead.

REPS: The Democrat candidate is a meanie.

Somebody, please ring the bell and call in the children. Recess must be over by now.

July 16, 2016

It is all a matter of respect.

I have never been an overtly religious person. I tend to keep my religious views private. But as I watch the news and read social media posts, it seems to me that if we were all to abide by ten simple rules maybe, just maybe, we could get along. These rules, written thousands of years ago, tell us, basically, to respect each other. It does not matter what one's religious belief is, or if he has none at all. Each religion, each philosophy, teaches us these same rules. They are:

1. You shall have no other gods before Me. (In other words, respect the universal truth that all religions teach.)

2. You shall not make false idols. (In other words, respect that universal truth more than you respect the celebrities or politicians you make into your gods.)

3. You shall not take the name of the LORD your God in vain. (In other words, respect your place in the greater order.)

4. Remember the Sabbath day, to keep it holy. (In other words, respect time to rest and reflect.)

5. Honor your father and your mother. (In other words, respect authority and the wisdom of those who came before you.)

6. You shall not murder. (In other words, respect each other.)

7. You shall not commit adultery. (In other words, respect your commitments.)

8. You shall not steal. (In other words, respect others' property.)

9. You shall not bear false witness against your neighbor. (In other words, respect the truth.)

10. You shall not covet. (In other words, respect yourself.)

It is all a matter of respect, after all.

July 17, 2016

I just finished re-reading the *Tao Te Ching*. The first stanza of Chapter 81 states:

"True words are not pleasing.

Pleasing words are not true.

Those who are right, do not argue.

Those who argue, are not right.

Those who know are not learned.

Those who are learned do not know."

~ (Lao Tzu - translated.)

My interpretation is that Lao Tzu warns against false speech and preaching. The truth is not always comfortable to hear, because it does not falsely flatter. But nor is it intentionally cruel. In today's society, political correctness is designed only to flatter and elicits no truth.

Too many people believe that the truth is relative, and we use that as an excuse to mold our words into something that can be accepted and praised by those from whom we seek approbation even when those words are not true. We use words to gain advantage and to promote our own agenda. We hide this by saying, *"It's only my opinion, and I am entitled to have and to share that opinion,"* but in so doing, we are not seeking solutions, answers or truth.

Too often, we hide our failures by hiding the truth. We claim to adhere to principles of tolerance and other ideals by telling white lies, cajoling and flattering, yet all too rarely are these words sincere in either thought or deed. Rather than elicit honest dialogue designed to shed light on issues and to promote truth, we use our words to obfuscate and hide that truth. Oh, yes, we may speak correctly, technically saying nothing that can be pointed to as false, and in that way hide what is real — what is true. We do this so much we do not even recognize when we do it.

We argue amongst ourselves to no purpose other than to argue. In that behavior, we only seek to promote our positions, and fail to promote truth.

Those of us who scream the loudest about this injustice or that do not seek a reasoned exchange of ideas, but rather seek only to drown out those thoughts or ideas with which we disagree. Those of us who scream the loudest do not seek justice, or knowledge, rather we seek to manipulate justice and to hinder knowledge. In so doing, the points we argue only seem more false.

We are right to question the motives of those who so aggressively seek to propagate their own position. When we call those with whom we disagree *"crooked"* or *"corrupt"* or use any other pejorative or denigrating word, we do so for only one purpose: to hide our own inadequacies. We only show our own corruption, our own crookedness.

When we fail to point out bad behavior whether that behavior is in word or in deed, or when we seek to flatter those we like by agreeing with their false premises solely for the purpose of currying favor, we hide the truth.

Fortunately, as Lao Tzu teaches, the truth will eventually prevail no matter the attempts at obfuscation.

Abraham Lincoln once paraphrased the bible in a famous speech when he said that a house divided against itself cannot stand.

For God's sake, we cannot even have discussions about issues without people screaming at each other and hurling insult as evidenced by so-called news programs and social media posts. Are we so mired in our own feelings about perceived injustice that we deem to be perpetrated against us (both real and imagined) that we are willing to destroy those who did not perpetrate the crime? The great American experiment is premised upon a belief that people can, with reasoned thought and debate, draw reasonable conclusions and form a social compact by which all could live.

When we withdraw from that compact, when we divide ourselves into us vs. them (regardless of who the *"us"* or who the *"them"* are);

When we forget that we are all Americans and that our common goals are to " . . . *establish justice, ensure domestic tranquility, provide for the common defense and promote the general welfare . . ."*;

When we cannot trust those institutions of our society to which we must turn to resolve our conflicts, because it seems the law favors only those who are rich enough to buy it or politically connected enough to divert it;

When we turn to our celebrities and our politicians as false idols then worship the ones we like as if they were the Second Coming, all the while concurrently denigrating those of whom we are not fond as if they were demons from hell bent solely on our destruction;

When we cannot turn to our neighbors with respect;

When we cannot even respect ourselves;

Then the house is so divided that it cannot stand.

I cannot help but wonder, are we witnessing the end of the American experiment?

July 19, 2016

Seeing the posts about a presidential candidate and his alleged statements about grabbing *"pussy,"* I cannot help but think . . .

The United States is 18-19 Trillion dollars in debt.

Unarmed black men are killed by police.

Police are being targeted by angry individuals.

The Zika virus has reached America's shores.

Greece is in chaos over their debt.—Britain is leaving the EU.

Russia is making military threats in and around Eastern Europe.

The Chinese are claiming the South China Sea, creating islands on which to build military bases, over protests of the Philippines, and with disregard to the ruling of the UN.

North Korea and Iran are attempting to build ballistic missiles and nuclear weapons.

ISIS is killing people all over the globe.

And, in the United States we are consumed with talk about "*pussy.*"

Nero fiddles and Rome burns.

JULY 20, 2016

Painting a group of people with a broad brush is stereotyping, discriminatory and bigoted; regardless of who is being painted by the brush. Claiming to be tolerant and denigrating people with whom we disagree is hypocritical.

July 16, 2016

I just finished reading George Orwell's *1984*. How prophetic! The similarities between Orwell's Oceania and the American dystopia today are striking.

Consider,

television screens that can watch what you do;

telephones that can listen in to your conversations;

a media that has turned hatred of others into an art form;

distortions, misinformation and flat out lies told by the government;

the changing of language such that previously innocuous words take on new meaning;

the re-writing of history to meet the current social and political ethos.

If you have not read this book, or if the last time you read it was while in high school, I urge you to read or re-read it. Then, turn on your television set and watch the so-called news. You, too, may be struck by the similarities in what you see on that set and Orwell's warnings.

July 17, 2016

It is another beautiful morning outside and, yet, I weep.

I weep for those who wait for a loved one that will never return.

I weep for those who fall victim to senseless loss of life over injustices both real and imagined.

I weep for those who have lost their love.

I weep for those who believe that name-calling is reasoned political thought.

I weep for those who graduate from our prestigious institutes of higher learning, yet remain uneducated.

I weep for those who have lost their minds.

I weep for those who have been so indoctrinated into dogmatic adherence to political ideologies that they are unwilling to even hear opposing viewpoints.

I weep for those who cannot listen.

I weep for those who have lost their ears.

I weep for those whose biases justify their vilifying anyone who does not share their viewpoint.

I weep for the hypocrites who are blind to their own hypocrisy.

I weep for those who have lost their eyes.

I weep for a citizenry that allows a political oligarchy to divide that citizenry into "*us*" and "*them*."

I weep for an electorate that cannot recognize the tactics of division.

I weep for those who have lost their way.

I weep for those so mired in narcissism they are unable to consider others.

I weep for a society hell-bent on its own destruction.

I weep for those who have lost their future.

I weep for our children.

It is another beautiful morning outside and, yet, I weep.

July 18, 2016

I just finished reading George Orwell's *Animal Farm*. Like with *1984*, it strikes me as so very prophetic.

In high school, we were taught that this work was a warning and indictment of the communist threat, but I see it as an indictment of any entrenched political class. The similarities between the pigs and what they did in the book and what is being done today by our own political oligarchy is striking.

Consider:

Like the pigs in this tome, there are those among us today who would rewrite history to suit their needs. In *Animal Farm*, when Snowball objected to the abuses of the elite, he was changed from a hero of the animal rebellion into a turncoat, traitor and vilified by his former friends. One can easily see how Americans today rewrite our past to change our heroes of that past into people that are vilified, because they did not follow what is the political ethos of today.

The pigs set aside land to be used for the retirement for animals when they reached a certain age. They promised specific rations of food to those retirees. But, the land and rations that had been set aside were instead put to other use. Can you say, "Social Security?"

The other animals blindly followed the pigs — after all, weren't the pigs smarter than they? The masses in our nation today blindly follow the political intelligentsia — after all, isn't the intelligentsia smarter than we?

When other animals questioned the inconsistencies of the pigs, they were vilified, brutalized and ultimately lost their lives. When people in our society today question the accepted political orthodoxy, they are vilified and brutalized. I wonder, how long will it be before we start losing our lives over objections to that orthodoxy?

The pigs re-wrote the seven animal commandments to suit their needs. For example, when the pigs began to drink alcohol, they changed *"Animals shall not drink alcohol"* into *"Animals shall not drink alcohol to excess"* — a change of the universal rule by which they had all agreed to live; a change made to suit the desire of the pigs to drink; a change made without consulting the other animals or obtaining their consent to that change. The other animals were barely the wiser. This seems very much like our entrenched political class today that changes rules to suit its needs or the current mores it wants to espouse. Of course, this is done without consulting the people or obtaining their consent to change those rules. Like the constituents of Animal Farm, we are barely the wiser.

The seven commandments ultimately were distilled into one: *"All animals are equal. But some animals are more equal than others."* Sounds very much like our current political culture, even if not so boldly stated.

By the end of the book, the animals on Animal Farm looked to their pig masters (who were meeting with their former human overlords) and they could not tell the difference between their prior oppressors and their current ones.

I wonder, can we?

I watch the news. I read the papers. I read the posts online.

What I see and hear are people who are: Against this person, this thing or this party.

What I do not see or hear are people who are: For this person, this thing or this party.

I cannot help but wonder, would we be better served by voting FOR something or someone rather than AGAINST?

As I read the internet posts that either intentionally, or out of a lack of research, spread misinformation and, sometimes, outright lies, usually because the person posting does not want to see or hear opposing viewpoints . . . I cannot help but to think of this quote:

"There are none so blind as those who will not see. The most deluded people are those who choose to ignore what they already know." ~1713 Works of Thomas Chalkley.

August 5, 2016

I am going to say something very controversial here, but before I do, please, everybody, take a deep breath, hold it in and then let it out slowly while counting to ten in your head.

Good, now, do it again . . . take a deep breath, hold it in and then let it out slowly while counting to ten in your head.

One more time . . . take a deep breath, hold it in and then let it out slowly while counting to ten in your head.

Now here is the controversial part:

Donald Trump is not the devil.

Hillary Clinton is not the devil.

Wait, wait, wait . . . take a deep breath, hold it in and then let it out slowly while counting to ten in your head.

I have never believed in demonic possession, but it seems that the mere mention of either of these names causes otherwise good, decent, intelligent people to froth at the mouth, speak in tongues and become apoplectic with rage.

Perhaps the country needs an exorcism.

August 6, 2016

As part of my "Revisiting the Classics Tour," last night, I finished reading Alduous Huxley's *Brave New World*. It was quite interesting. I have not really had time to marshal my thoughts on this one yet, but I did jot down a few notes:

The economics of conspicuous consumption is a virtue. It is excessive. *"Ending is better than mending,"* because mending means less consumption of new things. The old must be disposed of to make way for the new. This keeps the economy humming and the people happy. (Consider our society's current practice of disposable everything.)

Social mores are turned on their head. In Huxley's civilization, promiscuity is a virtue and monogamy is a vice. Monogamy leads to individual loyalties and the unfair taking of something that is meant to be shared by all. Promiscuity is promoted at a very early age and taught in the education centers. Everyone belongs to everyone. It is considered bad manners to fail to sleep with another. If you want someone, have them.

"Infantilism," i.e. seeking immediate gratification is considered good while delayed gratification is bad.

Immediate gratification leads to happiness. Delayed gratification leads to want.

The family unit is non-existent. The word *"father"* is a joke and the word *"mother"* a pejorative. Children are decanted in hatcheries (rather than born to parents) and are preconditioned through bio-chemical and genetic engineering and *"hypnopaedic"* sleep-induced conditioning to acceptance of their caste. Where one is content with one's lot and never aspires to anything greater, they are happy. It is Pavlovian conditioning; a cultural brainwashing through sleep induced interference that leads to utter happiness with no sadness. Sadness cannot exist because people are preconditioned to accept their lot and not want more than they are capable of obtaining. And if one does feel unhappy for whatever reason, there is always *"Soma"* — a narcotic with no ill side effects. Take a Soma vacation from your troubles and be happy. [This reminds me of a film we were shown in elementary school about the dangers of drugs — although, sometimes I think I could use a little Soma!]

Being alone is considered a vice. Everyone is encouraged to spend their time together and to never be alone a condition that is thought to be anti-social. After all, in this brave new world, alone-ness leads to thinking and thinking is a bad thing.

Reading is limited to how-to manuals and people are encouraged to go to the *"feelies"* (movies that enable the watcher to feel the effects on the screen). Books like the Bible, Shakespeare and/or anything written before the start of the new world order are banned. [Hmmm . . . maybe I will re-read Bradbury's *Fahrenheit 451* next.] History is destroyed. It is old and meaningless. Only the here and now matter. What need is there for history?

And this one part really caught my eye. I think it explains much about the human condition and why people behave the way they do:

"The mockery made him feel an outsider; and feeling an outsider he behaved like one, which increased the prejudice against him and intensified the contempt and hostility aroused by his physical defects. Which in turn increased his sense of being alien and alone."

What a keen insight into feelings of inferiority and the progression thereof that is!

I look around and, while we are not in Huxley's dystopia yet, I wonder are we on that path?

I cannot be the only one who wants to walk into a meeting (or any gathering) and just break out into that song by Jeannie C. Riley, "*Harper Valley PTA*".

August 11, 2016

We cause our children to read Bradbury's *Fahrenheit 451* and other books during high school, but I think high schoolers are too young to truly grasp the concepts. Children are narcissistic and see the world through a prism of that narcissism. It is not their fault. It is natural behavior. I know that I barely recall the things I read in this book some years ago. I think, it is not until we get older and we have life experiences behind us that we can fully appreciate the message in these tomes.

All I can say about *this* book is *"wow."* Originally published in 1951, I cannot help but wonder if Bradbury had a crystal ball. I am only half-way through it, but before page 55, I came across the following gems:

"Well, after all, this is the age of the disposable tissue. Blow your nose on a person, wad them, flush them away, reach for another, blow, wad, flush."

We are taught to value that which is rare and we are taught contempt for that which is abundant, In a world of six billion people, how are we to treat human life?

"Everyone I know is either shouting or dancing around like wild or beating up one another . Do you notice how people hurt each other nowadays? . . . I'm afraid of children my own age. They kill each other ."

How Prophetic! In 1951, we did not hear about children killing children. I am sure, it happened, but today it happens all too often.

"School is shortened, discipline relaxed, philosophies, histories, languages dropped, English and spelling gradually neglected, finally almost completely ignored. Life is immediate, the job counts, pleasure lies all about after work. Why learn anything save pressing buttons, pulling switches, fitting nuts and bolts?"

Wow — talk about the state of education and our need for immediate gratification!

"Don't step on the toes of the dog-lovers, the cat-lovers, doctors, lawyers, merchants, chiefs, Mormons, Baptists, Unitarians, second-generation Chinese, Swedes, Italians, Germans, Texans, Brooklynites, Irishmen, people from Oregon or Mexico . . . The bigger your market . . . the less you handle controversy . . . It didn't come from the Government down. There was no dictum, no declaration, no censorship, to start with, no! Technology, mass exploitation, and minority pressure carried the trick . . ."

Self-censorship run amok.

"We must all be alike. Not everyone BORN free and equal, as the Constitution says, but everyone MADE equal. Each man the image of every other; then all are happy, for there are no mountains to make them cower, to judge themselves against."

Failure to understand that it is equality of opportunity that matters — not equality of outcome.

"Colored people don't like Little Black Sambo. Burn it. White people don't feel good about Uncle Tom's Cabin. Burn it. Someone's written a book on tobacco and cancer of the lungs? The cigarette people are weeping? Burn the book."

The language in this quote alone would probably not be allowed today. Again, wow! All the issues surrounding political correctness and curbing so-called offensive speech wrapped nicely in a bow. If you don't like it, denigrate it, destroy it, don't let others see or hear it.

"If you don't want a house built, hide the nails and wood. If you don't want a man unhappy politically; don't give him two sides to a question to worry him; give him one. Better yet, give him none . . . give the people contests they win by remembering words to more popular songs . . . how much corn Iowa grew last year. Cram them full of non-combustible data, chock them so damned full of 'facts' they feel stuffed, but absolutely 'brilliant' with information. Then they'll feel they're thinking, they'll get a sense of motion without moving . . . Don't give them any slippery stuff like philosophy or sociology to tie things up with. That way lies melancholy."

How to manipulate people: give them facts but keep them from thinking. Keep the tools they need to think away from them.

I cannot wait to see what the rest of the book has to say.

August 12, 2016

I am struggling with how to say this:

Please respect each other.

I have many real-world friends and family. They run the gamut of all races, creeds, colors, national origins, genders and sexual orientations. There are many that are very liberal and many that are very conservative. Each and every man must choose for himself his own beliefs. I do not judge them for their views. How can I judge another when I have not walked in his shoes?

Good, decent people can and do disagree.

I love and support my real-world friends and family, not in spite of these differences, but because of them. If you are part of this group, I respect you. I expect you to respect each other. And, I would like to believe that you can respect me, too.

It is with a heavy heart, that I hear and/or read things by one member of my family and friends that denigrates another member — truly nasty comments about the supporters of one campaign or another; comments that are made without any consideration for the people they are denigrating; without knowing a single thing about that other person.

The crux of the issue here is not one's beliefs or opinions. It is the method by which people choose to express them. Why does anyone think it is ok to post nasty comments that serve no purpose other than to call those with whom they disagree names or otherwise question their morality or mental capacities? It makes me question my own judgment in these friendships, not because of the beliefs that are espoused, but because of the behavior used to express them.

I say to these family and friends, please stop. I love you, but I also love the people of whom you speak so ill. It is truly disrespectful and offensive.

When you do this, it does not diminish my feelings toward those you despise. It only diminishes my feelings toward you.

August 29, 2016

It's simple really. It's called respect.

I am not Jewish, but when I walk into a Synagogue, I wear a yarmulke.

I am not Catholic, but when I walk into a Church, I take off my hat.

I wear shoes and shirts in restaurants.

When I ask for something from a store clerk, a server at a restaurant, or anyone else who is responding to my request, I say, "*Please*" and "*Thank you*".

When on a bus or train and an elderly or disabled person, or a woman gets on, I offer my seat.

When I walk into a building, I hold the door for others around me.

I say, "*Sir*" and "*ma'am*".

When we disagree, I don't call you "*bigot*," "*racist*," "*asshole*," or "*idiot*." We simply disagree.

When in another country, I abide by their rules, laws and customs.

When at a sporting event and another country's team's national anthem is played, I stand.

When my country's national anthem is played, I stand and place my hand over my heart.

Why is it that those who scream loudest demanding respect, are the ones who so often fail to give it? Just because one has the legal right to do, or not do, something, does not mean he has the moral right.

It's simple really — it's called respect.

AUGUST 31, 2016

What the internet needs is more mothers monitoring their children's posts — whether the child is 7 or 57. If that person's mother would be embarrassed to say, "*Yes, that's how I raised him or her,*" maybe that person should reconsider the post.

SEPTEMBER 4, 2016

Things to do today:

Eat;

Pray;

Love;

Run over ex with car.

Why is that . . .

Those who clamor for tolerance . . . so often are the least tolerant of all;

Those who cry out for justice . . . so often are the least just;

Those who cry out for respect . . . so often are the last to show it;

Those who are the most easily offended . . . so often are the most offensive?

hy·poc·ri·sy (hə'päkrəsē/) noun: hypocrisy; plural noun: hypocrisies

1   the practice of claiming to have moral standards or beliefs to which one's own behavior does not conform; pretense.

In the days before cable news and alternative media outlets, most Americans received their news from the big three networks and/or from their local papers. With the advent of cable news and alternative media, people were able to turn to different sources.

A friend, recently told me that she never watches one of the cable news outlets, because, in her opinion, that outlet promotes propaganda and is nothing but a mouthpiece of the Republican Party. Moreover, she said, I should not watch that network, because I am poisoning my mind with that propaganda.

I explained to her that each morning, I watch each of the cable networks. Each day at lunch, I read news from various news organization's websites. Each evening, I watch the local news channels. In my opinion, each and every one of them are biased. It is telling that one network or another will report on the same story in vastly different ways. It is also quite telling to see what each network chooses to report or to omit from their reporting.

Journalism, you see, is dead. Today, what passes as *"journalism"* really is only opinion, viewpoint and biased reporting. It does not matter which organization does the *"reporting"*. The so-called reporting in our nation's pre-eminent newspapers fails the very basic tests of true journalism — the *"who, what, where, when, why and how"* of the story. Rather it's all spin about why the *"who"* is evil, why the *"what"* is wrong, why the *"where"* is irrelevant and, further, assigns the *"why"* and *"how"* motives based on pure speculation rather than fact finding.

So, I watch each of these networks. I read various papers and try to get my information from varied sources. Then, where possible, I research the stories on my own, so that I may make my own determination about what is being reported. I watch each of them to expose myself to different points of view. It is a shame, that so many people will only watch *"journalism"* that comports with their own preconceived notions.

For a democracy to thrive, the citizenry must be informed. They must be knowledgeable about the events and issues that face that democracy. They must be willing to expose themselves to different viewpoints and to feel unfettered in expressing their own — you, know, that pesky First Amendment right to freedom of speech. The citizenry must be willing to be tolerant of other viewpoints and to listen, really listen, to the other viewpoint not just dismiss it out of hand because they disagree and then resort to *ad hominem* attacks against those with whom they disagree. Reasoned, cogent thinking is what is needed. That thinking comes first from being informed about the facts, then considering the varied opinions that others have formed from those facts. It does not come by blind adherence to one's own prism of bias and prejudice.

Can democracy survive if opposing viewpoints are silenced?

To all of those who will not stand for the flag or national anthem:

Those who tout the Constitutional right of people to protest the national anthem or the flag of our nation are missing the point. Nobody disagrees that these individuals have the Constitutional right to so protest. They have an absolute Constitutional right to do so and nobody would take that right away, but . . .

Those who fail to show respect for the flag and the anthem simply do not understand what they represent.

That flag, that anthem represents the blood, sweat and tears of a people who declared that *"all men are created equal"* and that they are *"endowed by their creator with certain inalienable rights, that among these are life, liberty and the pursuit of happiness."*

That flag, that anthem was borne of and represents the blood, sweat and tears of a people who upon making that declaration fought valiantly to throw off the yoke of an oppressive monarchy and to establish a representative democracy in this *"New World."*

That flag, that anthem represents the blood, sweat and tears of a people who declared that a people have the right to self-determination.

That flag, that anthem represents the blood, sweat and tears of a people who endured the horrors of civil war to free a portion of its people from the bonds of slavery.

That flag, that anthem represents the blood, sweat and tears of a people who not only fought for their own freedoms, but who twice entered the fray of world war to free the peoples of Europe from the imperial designs of its ruling classes.

That flag, that anthem represents the blood, sweat and tears of a people who, during that second world war, opposed the imperial ambitions of one Asian nation against its neighbors.

That flag, that anthem represents the blood, sweat and tears of a people who went through the trying times of civil discord to enact civil rights that would be applicable to all.

That flag, that anthem represents the blood, sweat and tears of a people who entered a cold war to thwart the ambitions of a political system that would deny people the basic freedom to choose their own leaders.

That flag, that anthem represents the blood, sweat and tears of a people who went to the Middle East in the 1990s and ejected a maniacal dictator from the borders of Kuwait.

That flag, that anthem represents the blood, sweat and tears of a people who went again into Europe to free the peoples of Bosnia/Serbia.

That flag, that anthem represents the blood, sweat and tears of a people who are not perfect, but who strive toward the perfection of their ideals — even if we often fail.

That flag, that anthem represents the very Constitutional right that people use to protest it.

It is not our successes that we honor when we show respect for that banner or that song . . . it is our continual, valiant attempts to, despite those failures, move toward the perfection of the ideals expressed by our Founding Fathers so long ago.

Yes, those who would protest that flag, that anthem, declaring them to be symbols of oppression and malfeasance have an absolute Constitutional right to do so, and I, for one, would never take that away from them.

But I wonder, do they understand what it is they are protesting?

SEPTEMBER 10, 2016

It is so hard to believe that it has been fifteen years since that fateful day in 2001 — the day that changed the world forever.

Like millions of people across the world, I sat in horror that Tuesday morning watching the events that unfolded in New York, DC and Pennsylvania. Words cannot begin to describe the emotions that I felt; that all Americans were feeling. Every year, as the memorials air on television, I cannot help but weep.

I weep for the losses on that day, but, for me, there is so much more to September 11 than those vicious attacks. You see, on that day, as the nation was glued to their television sets watching the horror, that was taking place, my mother was at work in Austin some 1,500 miles away from the events. She grasped her head, fell, and never woke again. That was the day that my life changed. It was an aneurysm, they said.

I was living in Philadelphia. I was young — only thirty-five years old and still struggling to find the man that I would become. Unable to catch a flight, train or bus, I packed my bags, got in my car and made the 33-hour trek across the country to be with my mother. It was the wee hours of Friday morning before I finally got to the hospital room. But she was not there. In her place was but an empty shell. I knew then, that my life would never be the same. How would I ever find the man I could become without her wisdom and guidance?

As a child, she taught me many things: to stand on my own two feet; to work hard; to try and always do the right thing — even if, sometimes, I fail.

She taught me to love, to laugh; to care for others and to be soft when I needed to be soft.

She taught me to stand up for myself and to be hard when I needed to be hard.

I remember, as a child, having a 102 degree fever, but still made to sit at the table with the family during dinner. This taught me that we each have responsibilities that we must live up to; there are things that we <u>must</u> do, no matter how we feel or how hard the doing.

I remember how, as all children do, I would sometimes fall down and get a "*boo-boo*". Most mothers kiss the "*boo-boo*" or give the child a cookie to make them feel better, but not Maria. She told me to "*go do it again, so you learn not to.*" Well, I learned "*not to.*" And through this, she taught me to overcome my failures and to learn from them.

I remember saying to her, "*I love you, Mom,*" and her reply . . . "*I love you too, or I wouldn't put up with your shit.*" Through this, she taught me that love is not words, but actions.

She was a strong woman and she taught me to be strong.

It was three months before I was really able to cry over that loss. I was in shock; numbed by everything; lost and uncertain about the path forward. But I remembered the things that she taught me. And so, I put one foot in front of the other and kept moving forward.

In the ensuing months and years, I reflected back on those days and the many days before. I remembered the lessons she taught me and realized how much I learned from her. Since those dark days, by thinking of her, I have learned to laugh and smile again.

Fifteen years ago, some evil men, knocked down two towers in the midst of Manhattan, but they could not destroy the foundation upon which those buildings stood. Today, a beautiful memorial stands in their place — a reminder of the human spirit.

Fifteen years ago, some evil thing knocked down this towering woman. But it could not destroy the foundation upon which she taught me to stand. Today, I hope that I make her proud and that I stand in memorial to her — a reminder of her beautiful spirit.

September 10, 2016

The Underwear Zone

When you are very young, you don't care about how you dress. You will go anywhere in your underwear.

When you are a teenager, all you care about is how you dress. You would not go outside in only your underwear.

When you are in your twenties, you would not go out unless you are have clean underwear to show off at the club.

When you are in your thirties, you would not be seen in your underwear unless it's "*sexy.*"

When you are in your forties, you do not care as long as your underwear is comfortable.

In your fifties, you go to the mailbox in just your underwear and you don't care what they look like.

As you get older, your underwear zone gets bigger.

It won't be too much longer, now, until I am going to the grocery store in just my boxers.

In *The Art of War*, Sun Tzu wrote:

"If your enemy is secure at all points, be prepared for him. If he is in superior strength, evade him. If your opponent is temperamental, seek to irritate him. Pretend to be weak, that he may grow arrogant. If he is taking his ease, give him no rest. If his forces are united, separate them. If sovereign and subject are in accord, put division between them. Attack him where he is unprepared, appear where you are not expected." ~ Sun Tzu, *The Art of War.*

Today, I saw one post calling Trump supporters *"idiots"* and another calling Clinton supporters *"stupid."*

According to the latest polls, Clinton and Trump are neck-and-neck. About half of the country supports one, while the other half of the country supports the other. So, according to these posts, about half of Americans are *"idiots"* while the other half of Americans are *"stupid."*

Sun Tzu wrote: *"If his forces are united, separate them. If sovereign and subject are in accord, put division between them."*

And, thus, we defeat ourselves.

September 11, 2016

Great empires are not felled by the arms of their enemies. Generally, the military prowess of the empire is too strong to be overcome by direct attack. Rather, they are felled by a rot within. This has been true of all empires throughout the history of civilization — Babylon, Persia, Egypt, Alexander, Rome, and on and on.

It is a rot that pervades when the civilization becomes so drunk on its own superiority that it loses respect for even those institutions that made it great.

It is a rot that pervades when the people no longer trust the very institutions they put in place to protect themselves.

It is a rot that pervades when the people turn to their celebrities for answers and away from the very institutions that once provided them.

It is a rot that pervades the body politic; a ruling class that ignores the will of the people.

It is a rot that pervades when its people turn away from the things that made it a great empire to start with — its art, its culture, its mores, its society.

It is a rot that pervades when the spark of petty squabbles become gross conflagrations.

It is a rot that pervades when its people turn on each other.

Great empires are not felled by the arms of their enemies. Generally, the military prowess of the empire is too strong to be overcome by direct attack. Rather, they are felled by a rot within. This has been true of all empires throughout the history of civilization — Babylon, Persia, Egypt, Alexander, Rome, and on and on.

Do we believe that today is different? History only repeats itself.

My knee has gone out, my wrist is in pain, my back is sore. I have the sniffles and a headache . . .

It must be Monday.

September 13, 2016

My knee is still out, my wrist is still hurting, my back is better, but my neck is sore. The sniffles and the headache are gone. I only rose twice to go the bathroom last night.

It must be Tuesday.

September 14, 2016

Does anyone else suffer from lucid dreams? (For those who do not know what they are, they are dreams you have while knowing that you are asleep.) I have had lucid dreams almost my entire life. They are almost always the same dream with slight variations: I am lying in bed and unable to get up. Someone (or something) is either at the foot of my bed, standing next to the bed or hovering over me. It is clear that he, she or it means me harm. I know that I am asleep, but I cannot wake myself. I thrash around trying to wake — looking like Linda Blair in *"The Exorcist."* But of course, this is only happening in my mind. In reality, I am asleep in bed not moving at all.

Just the other night, a clown (and, yes [sorry clowns] I believe that **all** clowns are evil) was leaning over me, trying to pull the pillow from underneath my head. I think that he intended to smother me with it. He even knew that I was aware that I was sleeping. He wore a malicious grin that showed this knowledge. He knew that I knew it was a dream and that I could not stop him! (Remember Freddy Krueger?)

It was quite some time before I learned how to wake myself from these nightmares, and, now, I can do it fairly easily. But the dreams are still frightening.

Do I need a psychiatrist, an exorcist or just to participate in a sleep study?

When a civilization's culture becomes so crude that bad behavior is considered acceptable in the name of individual rights;

When people use their individual right to freedom of expression not as a means of expressing themselves in a reasoned manner, but as an excuse to behave in a boorish way;

When that boorish behavior becomes acceptable to the point that it is the norm;

When it becomes normal for celebrities to disrespect individuals or institutions with whom they disagree;

When a populace becomes so enamored with its celebrities that it excuses that celebrity's bad behavior;

When that populace finds ways to avoid the consequences of bad behavior rather than avoid the bad behavior itself;

When bad behavior is not frowned upon, but instead it is celebrated;

That civilization is on the decline.

Yes, each of us has the right to behave badly. It does not mean that we should.

SEPTEMBER 19, 2016

I regularly see a meme on Facebook to the effect that, *"back in the day"* a family could survive on one income, but that today, a family needs two incomes to maintain the same standard of living. Well, this is not exactly true, is it?

A family can still survive on one income today. It is all a matter of the choices we make.

You see, *"back in the day,"*

Generally, the father went to work and the mother stayed home.

We did not order take-out food or delivery and going to a restaurant was a rare treat, indeed. Meals, you see, were cooked at home and the family sat together at the table during dinner-time. If you want to live on one income, cook your meals at home, eschew take-out, delivery and go to restaurants only on special occasions. After all, it costs a lot less.

We did not hire people clean the house. The stay-at-home mom took care of that. Each child had his specific chores for which he was responsible. If you want to live on one income, clean the house yourself with the assistance of the entire family. After all, it costs a lot less.

The stay-at-home mom cared for the children. We did not hire babysitters, daycare or nannies. If you want to live on one income, raise your own children. After all, it costs a lot less.

The stay-at-home mom ironed the clothes. There was no need to take the shirts to the cleaners. If you want to live on one income, iron your own clothes. After all, it costs a lot less.

We did not have gardeners to take care of our lawn. Once a week, dad and the kids were out in the yard. If you want to live on one income, do your own yard work. After all, it costs a lot less.

A family had one phone line, generally in the kitchen, shared by everyone. We did not have multiple cell phones, data plans and the accompanying bills. If you want to live on one income, get rid of your cell phone and live with one phone in the house. After all, it costs a lot less.

A family had one television. We watched only the channels that were available on the *"free"* airwaves. If you want to live on one income, get rid of cable. After all, it costs a lot less.

We did not have the internet and the accompanying bills. If you want to live on one income, get rid of the internet — go the library if you must go online. After all, it costs a lot less.

The children shared bedrooms and there was one bathroom in the house. If you want to live on one income, get a smaller house. After all, it costs a lot less.

We did not schedule every minute of the day with appointments for our children. There was no incessant soccer practice, band practice, play dates, piano lessons. We did not have a *"teen space"* in the house. We did not have x-box, playstation, etc. For entertainment, we went outside to play. If you want to live on one income, send the kids outside to play. After all, it costs a lot less.

My brother and I shared one bicycle. If you want to live on one income, share your toys. After all, it costs a lot less.

A family can still survive on one income today. It is only a matter of the choices that we make. If we want to live on one income, make wiser choices.

After all, it costs a lot less.

SEPTEMBER 20, 2016

"The fourth estate is a term that positions the press (newspapers) as a fourth branch of government and one that is important to a functioning democracy."

This phrase is attributed to Edmund Burke (1729 — 1797), a British politician, as quoted in Thomas Carlyle's book, *"Heroes and Hero Worship in History"* (1841).

Burke said that there were three Estates in Parliament, but in *"the Reporters Gallery yonder, there sat a fourth Estate more important far than they all."*

An informed electorate is a necessary precursor for a functioning democracy. A thriving democracy rests on the foundation of that electorate. But what happens when that fourth estate abdicates its duty to responsible, honest journalism and instead becomes a mouthpiece for one political party or another, or one candidate or another? What happens when a populations chooses to get their news from that single source?

When a *"news"* network selectively edits the comments of its guests, that network is abdicating its responsibility for honest journalism. If the media is unwilling or unable to tell the truth, our democracy is at risk.

This November, the nation is faced with a choice wherein each of the candidates from the major political parties appear to be, shall we say, challenged with the truth. In this environment, it is incumbent upon our political media to be vigilant in honestly reporting the facts.

I urge each and every one of you to read George Orwell's "*Animal Farm*" and "*1984.*" Then, watch the news (each of the networks, it does not really matter which one). Then **re-**read George Orwell's books for good measure.

Then ask yourself . . . is this where we are?

Some Germans were responsible for the murder of Jews, gays, gypsies and other minority groups. Some Germans tried to protect others from that regime. Would you paint all Germans with a broad brush?

Some Russians got fat on the backs of exploited workers. Some Russians fought against that communist regime. Would you paint all Russians with a broad brush?

Some people in some Asian countries engaged in the sex-slave trade. Some people in those Asian countries fought against that. Would you paint all Asians with a broad brush?

Some people in some African nations to this day, still sell women into slavery. Some people in those African nations fight against that. Would you paint all Africans with a broad brush?

Some Muslims engage in acts of terrorism. Some Muslims fight against that. Would you paint all Muslims with a broad brush?

And, yes, some Americans shoot innocent men and women. Some Americans fight against that. Would you paint all Americans with a broad brush?

In America, the people who fight against oppression and tyranny do so under the banner of the American flag and sing our national anthem. Those symbols stand for that fight. As a people, we are not perfect. We are constantly striving to reach our ideals as expressed in the Declaration of Independence and in the Constitution. Some people, misunderstand those ideals. Some people work against them. But as a nation, as a people we are constantly striving to do better.

Those symbols do not represent perfection. They represent the fight for perfection.

Those who proclaim that those symbols are symbols of oppression do not understand the symbols.

In response to a Facebook post that opined that all wars have been started by men . . .

Cleopatra started wars in partnership with Mark Anthony. The Queen of the Iceni went to war against Rome. Zenobia of Palmyra also went to war against war as did Boudicca. Aefelflaed (the '*Lady of the Mercians*')fought against the Danes. Matilda of Tuscany fought against the Austrian Emperor. Joan of Arc did not start a war, but she participated in one. Margaret of Anjou fought for her husband King Henry VI of England. Lakshmibai (the Valiant Rani) queen of Jhansi, fought against the British in the Indian Mutiny. Queen Elizabeth I, Catherine the Great . . .

These woman might be surprised to find out they were actually men in drag.

September 23, 2016

We riot when we're happy,
We riot when we're sad,
We riot when we feel sappy,
We riot when we're mad.

We riot when we protest,
Against harm that has been done,
Our riots will continue,
Until the war is won.

It doesn't really matter,
Why we riot on today,
Incessant, endless chatter,
Will carry all the way.

We riot not to prove a point,
Or protest what we see,
We riot because we're out of joint,
Now listen to our plea.

We riot and our slogans chant,
Who cares if words are true,
We riot and we show our slant,
Our bias against you.

We riot for the things we've not,
And for things that would appeal,
We riot and we show our rot,
When we maim and steal.

We riot so to take from those,
Who have, but will not share,
It matters not who strikes the blows,
We riot 'cause it's there.
Our riots aren't to show we're right,
Or that we have no job,
We riot so to show our might,
The power of the mob.

Mario Kiefer

We riot when we're happy,
We riot when we're sad,
We riot when we feel sappy,
We riot when we're mad.

SEPTEMBER 24, 2016

I saw a post proclaiming that it is *"Gay Uncles Day"* and I
wondered when Hallmark will create the

*"Please-Stop-Making-Up-Holidays-To-Celebrate-Every-Damn-
Thing-In-Life-Because-We-Are-Rich-Enough-And-Don't-Need-
Ya'll-To-Buy-Any-More-Damn-Holiday-Cards"* Day.

Once upon a time, in a Land far, far away . . .

The Land was built upon Universal Truth and was populated by a tribe of many Selves. The Selves belonged to varied Families who in turn belonged to varied Clans who made up the body of the Tribe. Regardless of the Self, Family or Clan, all understood that the foundation of the Land was Universal Truth. They had many languages and they called the Universal Truth by many names - Jehovah, Allah, Karma, Mother Nature, God. Regardless of what they called it, they understood it to be one thing.

The Selves of the Tribe further understood that the way to peace and harmony was to subordinate their divisions. And so they worshipped in that order — first at the Altar of the Universal Truth, then at the Altar of the Tribe, the Altar of the Clan, the Altar of the Family and finally at the Altar of the Self.

The Universal Truth had Ten Precepts by which the Selves were governed — don't kill, cheat, steal, covet, etc. If each Self lived in accordance with the Ten Precepts, they could worship at the altar of Universal Truth perfectly and the Land would flourish. The Ten Precepts were written in stone and placed in the Great Hall for all to see and come to know.

But there was no enforcement in this life for the Ten Precepts. The Selves were fallible, you see and Universal Truth did not punish those who strayed. And as is the way of these things, it came to pass that the various Selves of the Tribe noticed that too often those who refused to follow the Ten Precepts flourished and prospered at the expense of others. This was unjust, they cried and fought among themselves. So, the Tribal Elders passed "Justice" so that all might live in peace and harmony. The members of the Tribe thanked their Elders and called Justice good. They placed Justice above the Ten Precepts in the Great Hall so that all might see and come to know Justice. They turned their back on the Universal Truth and began to first worship at the Altar of the Tribe.

But the Tribal Elders, who each were Selves and members of the varied Clans, were fallible, you see. And as is the way of these things, it came to pass that the Clans noticed that too often those Clans who refused to follow Justice flourished and prospered at the expense of other Clans. The Clans fought amongst themselves. So, they turned to their Clan Guardians and demanded "The Law". Each of the Clans then passed The Law so that all might live in peace and harmony. The members of the Clans thanked their respective Guardians and called The Law good. And within the Great Hall, they placed The Law above Justice which in turn was placed above the Ten Precepts so that all might see and come to know The Law. They turned their backs on Justice and began to first worship at the Altar of the Clan.

But the Clan Guardians, who each were Selves and members of the varied Families, were fallible. And as is the way of these things, it came to pass that the Families noticed that too often those Families who refused to follow The Law flourished and prospered at the expense of other Families. The Clans seemed unable to enforce The Law. This is unfair, they cried and turned to their Family Patriarchs and demanded "Fairness." Each of the Families then passed Fairness so that all might live in peace and harmony. The members of the various Families thanked their Patriarchs and called Fairness good. And in the Great Hall, they placed Fairness above The Law, which in turn was placed above Justice, which in turn was placed above the Ten Precepts so that all might see and come to know Fairness. They turned their backs on the Law and began to first worship at the Altar of the Family.

But the Family Patriarchs, who each were Selves, were fallible. And as is the way of these things, it came to pass that the Selves noticed that too often those Selves who refused to follow Fairness flourished and prospered at the expense of other Selves. The Families seemed unable to enforce Fairness. It seemed wrong. So, to fight the wrong, they demanded "Rights." Each Self was responsible for his own Rights. They put forth their Rights and placed them within the Great Hall above Fairness, which in turn was above The Law, which in turn was above Justice, which in turn was above the Ten Precepts so that all might see and come to know Rights. They turned their backs on the Families and began to worship at the Altar of the Self.

But the Selves were fallible. And as is the way of these things, it came to pass that the Selves argued and fought with each other over whose Rights were more important —

whose Rights were paramount and who could or would enforce those Rights. They took to the streets. They followed no Precepts, they practiced Justice. They followed no Law and forgot about Fairness. They worshipped solely at the Altar of Rights.

And as is the way of these things, it came to pass that the Land was destroyed.

For you see,

In the Land where the Self is worshipped before the Family, there can be no Fairness;

In the Land where the Family is worshipped before the Clan, there can be no Law;

In the Land where the Clan is worshipped before the Tribe, there can be no Justice; and,

In the Land without Universal Truth, regardless of which of the many names you choose to call it — Jehovah, Allah, Karma, Mother Nature, God . . .

. . . There is nothing.

SEPTEMBER 27, 2016

On last night's Presidential debate:

It was, as I feared. Each of the candidates appeared as children on the playground — calling each other names and offering no real solutions. Each of the candidates appeared smug, arrogant and entitled. Neither seemed very presidential to me.

I am not an economist, but I know this: you cannot spend more than you earn and expect not to go bankrupt; and the political class does nothing.

I am not a military expert, but I know this: you cannot defeat your enemy, if you are unwilling to fight; and the political class does nothing.

I am not a climatologist, but I know this: you cannot have clean air and water if you continue to pollute; and the political class does nothing.

I am not an energy expert, but I know this: you cannot power the nation on sources that do not provide sufficient energy to fulfill your needs; and the political class does nothing.

I am not an investment banker, but I know this: you cannot invest in companies that go bankrupt; and the political class does nothing.

I am not an expert on infrastructure, but I know this: when you have already paid for repairs, the item should be fixed; and the political class does nothing.

I am not an expert on transparency, but I know this: you cannot claim transparency when you hide; and the political class does nothing.

I am not an expert on prejudice, but I know this: you cannot solve bias, by creating more bias; and the political class does nothing.

I am not an expert on foreign aid, but I know this: you cannot give to another to fix his house, when your own home is in disrepair; and the political class does nothing.

I am not an expert on immigration, but I know this: when a pipe bursts in your basement and it is flooded, you cannot simply bail out water — you must fix the leak; and the political class does nothing.

I am not an expert on tax policy, but I know this: you cannot claim that all must pay their *"fair share"* then enact loopholes for everyone to avoid paying; and the political class does nothing.

I am not an expert on anything, but I know this: the rich get richer, the poor get poorer; and the political class does nothing.

The great ship of America is sinking; and the political class does nothing.

OCTOBER 2, 2016

There are thirty-seven days until the election and the choices could not be more stark. Be sure to get out there and vote one way or the other.

It is up to you to choose whether . . .

to make the Democrat's friends richer

or

to make the Republican's friends richer.

Vote.

One of my friends recently complained that she was stopped by the police and given a ticket.

I asked, *"What was the ticket for?"*

"Speeding," she replied.

"Were you speeding?" I asked.

"Yes," she said, *"but . . ."*

But? But, what?

If you are speeding, and you are stopped by the police and given a ticket for speeding, pay the ticket. There is no *"but."*

It seems to me, that we all want what we want, **BUT** don't want to be responsible for our wants.

We want to be in better health, **BUT** we don't want to give up bad food, alcohol, tobacco, etc.

We want to live in a smoke free society, **BUT** only as it pertains to tobacco; we want to light up our doobie anytime and anywhere.

We want to be in better shape, **BUT** we don't want to work out.

We want to make more money, **BUT** we don't want to pay for an education.

We want to work for our money, **BUT** we only want to work in a "*creative*" field.

We want to make a livable wage, **BUT** we only want to work part-time.

We want everyone to be tolerant, **BUT** we don't want to hear opposing points of view.

We want what we want, **BUT** . . .

The problem with our society is all of the **BUTS** . . . Don't be a **BUT**.

OCTOBER 3, 2016

I remember as a child coming home from school and feeling very frustrated over something that had happened. I said the word *"dammit."* My mother overheard me and promptly washed out my mouth with soap. She told me, that she did this, because I had used a *"dirty"* word and she had to clean my mouth thereafter.

Well, it happened that the next day, I came home from school and told my mother that I didn't like *"Billy"* because *"Billy"* was a *"jerk."* She promptly took me over her knee and gave me a good whipping.

Now, I understood that the word *"dammit"* was a dirty word and that is why my mouth was washed out with soap. But the word *"jerk"* was not a bad word, was it? So, why did I get a whipping? I asked my mother why the word *"dammit"* got my mouth washed out with soap, but the word *"jerk"* got me an even worse punishment — a spanking?

Calmly, she explained:

You are known by what you do.

You are known by what you say.

You are known by what others hear and see.

I am known by what you do.

I am known by what you say.

I am known by what others hear and see from you.

It doesn't matter if the word is in and of itself a *"dirty"* word — what matters is how you use it. You should never use any word with the sole intent of demeaning or belittling another. Doing so does not demean that other person, but rather demeans you. Your actions; your words reflect not only on you, but on the one who raised you.

To those who would call others *"asshole," "bitch," "stupid," "idiot"* — or whatever word is being used, do you ever ask yourself:

How am I known? How is my mother known?

OCTOBER 4, 2016

A friend of mine just received a check from a class action lawsuit. My friend's *pro rata* share of the settlement — ten cents. It cost more to mail the check, then the check itself.

I wonder how much the attorneys' fees were?

Early in the days of the Republic, our forefathers granted authority to the federal government to establish a common currency — dollars and cents. They gave the federal government the power to tax; to raise revenue; to pay the common bills; to do all those things that the federal government had responsibility to do.

As time wore on, it became apparent that the federal government needed to increase revenue. So, an amendment to the Constitution was passed that gave the federal government the authority to institute an income tax; to raise more common dollars and cents to pay the common bills out of a common fund.

As time wore on, the federal government spent more and more of that common revenue on things that, well, were not so common at all. They spent the common funds on frivolous pursuits, on things for which there was no Constitutional authority for them to spend, and on their friends or helping special interest groups. Let's be clear, common funds were being spent on things that did not benefit the common people, but only benefitted the special interests. Our common funds were no longer spent on common interest.

When will we return to common dollars spent on common goals? When will return to common cents?

OCTOBER 5, 2016

The Art of the Left Handed Compliment

A left-handed compliment is defined as a compliment with two meanings, one of which is unflattering to the receiver, and to which the receiver can hardly object.

Nobody has perfected the art of the left handed compliment as well as *"polite society"* in the South. Here are a few of my favorites:

I wish that I could look as good as you do and weigh that much.

I love that dress, every time you wear it.

How brave you are to go out with no makeup.

If my children were as behaved as yours, I would be on my knees everyday thanking the Lord for His guidance.

I love that shirt, it's so retro.

That dress is so hip and trendy, I wish I could get away with wearing something like that.

That haircut is so slimming to your face.

You are so competent for someone so inexperienced.

I wish that I had known as much at your age.

Responding to someone who said, "*I feel old and fat*": "*You are not old.*"

OCTOBER 6, 2016

To those who advocate raising the tax rate on the wealthy . . . in the words of Hillary Clinton: "*What difference does it make?*"

We can tax people at 90%, but so long as we have a tax code that enables people to use loopholes and deductions that cut their effective tax rate to zero, it does not matter to what level we raise the rate.

I received my DNA results today. Turns out I am:

1% Angel

1% Devil

98% Human

This means that:

Although, sometimes I do good and sometimes I do evil, usually I just try my best, but am prone to mistakes.

October 8, 2016

When I walk into a convenience store to purchase some goodies and hand the clerk the money, he does not care what brand I am purchasing. Nor does he care whether I hand him the coin heads or tails up. The brand is irrelevant to his sale and the coin has two sides; each of which spends just as easily.

When Special Interest walks into a convenience store to purchase some goodies and hands the clerk the money, the clerk does not care what political party that Special Interest is purchasing. Nor does he care whether the coin is heads or tails up. The party is irrelevant to his sale and the coin has two sides; each of which spends just as easily.

One day in January 2017,

You will wake from a fretful sleep, having been up half the night fretting over the worries of the day.

You will make lunch for your children and send them off to school to get in inadequate education.

You will go to work at a job you most likely do not enjoy — or if you have no job, presumably you will be looking for one.

You will pay your mortgage or rent and all your other bills, then look down at your balance sheet and wonder how you do it.

You will eat too much food as you worry about your diet.

Somewhere, one group or another will be protesting one thing or another.

Somewhere, there will be a terrorist attack by some group or another.

Some nation or another will take menacing and provocative actions against another.

Congress will spend more money than the government takes in, and the nation's debt will expand.

Congressmen will spend more time with lobbyists and fundraisers than they will on solving the nation's problems.

Either Clinton or Trump will be sworn in as the new president.

And on the next day . . . nothing will change.

OCTOBER 12, 2016

We recognize a man by his good works. We see and hear his performance and give him accolades and applause.

But a great man, is seldom seen or heard, because he does his good works behind closed door and seeks no recognition.

With all of the political wisdom being shared on social media each and every day, I wonder, how many people can (without looking it up or googling it) name:

The two US Senators from their state;

The Congressman that represents them in the US House of Representatives.

October 14, 2016

As a child, I would climb into the back of my mother's car and ask her, *"Where are we headed?"*

Her reply, *"To Hell if we don't change our ways."*

As an adult, I watch the news and see the mean-spirited posts on social media and I ask myself, *"Where are we headed?"*

"Yesterday is but a dream,

Tomorrow is only a vision.

But today well lived

makes every yesterday a dream of happiness,

and every tomorrow a vision of hope." ~Kalidasa, *The Complete Works of Kalidasa*

To which, I add:

Help me, Lord, to live this day well.

October 15, 2016

You want tolerance so badly, that you denigrate those who are not tolerant.

You want love so badly, that you hate those who do not love.

You want justice so badly, that you are willing to commit a crime to get it.

You want peace so badly, that you are willing to commit violence for it.

Do your actions bring about the goal you seek or in the acting, do you destroy the goal?

Yesterday, a friend posted a cute picture of a kitten, sitting on its hind legs, its fore legs up and its beautiful soulful eyes gazing at the camera. Someone commented on the post that the picture was contrived. In order to get the kitten to pose in that manner, they said, the kitten was forced to beg for food. It was animal cruelty and offensive.

Hmmmm. . .

To me, the most offensive thing in our political discussions these days is the use of the word "*offensive.*" This is so, because those who are so "*offended*" generally use that word not because they are truly offended by the thing that is being said or shown, but rather as a means to silence speech and cut off debate.

I ask:

In a society where some *body* is offended by some *thing*, some *where* at some *time*, and *every* thing is offensive to *some* body, *some* where at *some* time, and where we silence speech that *some body* deems offensive at *some time*, *some where*, can we even communicate let alone have open intelligent and robust debate?

We are told:

Don't talk about politics — somebody might get offended.

Don't talk about sex — somebody might get offended.

Don't talk about religion —somebody might get offended.

Don't talk about the latest hurricane, earthquake, tornado or other part of the weather — somebody adversely effected by same might get offended.

Don't wear Halloween costumes that reflect another's culture — somebody might get offended.

Don't talk about anything — somebody might get offended.

And, for God's sake, whatever you do, don't post a picture of a kitten!

Use of impure means to obtain a pure goal cheapens the goal. It does not matter if what you seek is good and pure, if you employ evil methods, your goal no longer is.

The ends do not justify the means.

OCTOBER 19, 2016

rac·ism (rā̠sizəm/)

The belief that all members of each race possess characteristics or abilities specific to that race, especially so as to distinguish it as inferior or superior to another race or races.

So many of us need to read and understand this definition.

OCTOBER 20, 2016

On Tuesday, November 8, 2016, Americans will make a choice.

Given the current state of politics, I am not at all certain whether the choice will be for the Democrat or Republican nominee.

Given the current state of politics, I am certain that whatever the choice, the United States will be poorer for it.

Most people stick with the flavor they grew up with. If you grew up drinking cherry Kool-Aid, you will continue to drink cherry Kool-Aid. If you grew up drinking lemon-flavored Kool-Aid, you will continue to drink lemon-flavored Kool-Aid. Sometimes people switch their preference when they get older, finding one flavor or the other too sweet, too tart, too . . . whatever. Regardless of the preference, they are still drinking Kool-Aid.

Most people stick with the political party they grew up with. If you grew up in a Democratic household, you will continue to be a Democrat. If you grew up in a Republican household you will continue to be a Republican. Sometimes people switch their preference when they get older, finding one party or the other too liberal, too conservative, too . . . whatever.

Regardless of the preference, they are still drinking the Kool-Aid.

October 22, 2016

The only thing I find more disturbing than those who are unwilling to consider differing points of view, are those who are unwilling even to listen to them.

OCTOBER 23, 2016

Ok . . . before you read this, don't get your panties in a wad. It's called a joke. What makes a joke funny is that it has a kernel of truth to it. And I find this one funny. If you think about it, you may too.

What is the difference between a "*slut*" and a "*bitch*"?

A "*slut*" sleeps with everyone.

A "*bitch*" sleeps with everyone . . . but <u>you</u>.

Mario Kiefer

Newton's Third Law of Motion states, *"For every action there is an equal and opposite reaction."*

Is there any reason to believe that this does not apply to human interaction as well?

In an ancient Roman province, a man was charged with crimes against the Roman State. There were no facts to support the allegations of criminal activity, but the political, social and religious elites who formed the ruling class of the province were threatened by his existence. So they brought him before the Roman governor of the province and demanded that he be executed. Only the governor had the authority to order such punishment.

The Roman governor listened to the complaints of the elites and pointed out that there were no facts to support the allegations. The elites lied and argued that the truth was that the man was a threat to the stability and welfare of the state. And the people, believing the lie, supported their elites and repeated that lie.

The governor again pointed out that there were no facts to support the charge of criminal activity. But the elites grew more fervent in their condemnation. Again, they lied. *"The truth,"* they said, *"is that he is a threat to the stability and welfare of the state."* And, the people, believing the lie, grew more fervent and supported their elites in repeating the lie.

So, the governor, whose principal charge was to keep the peace, relented. He gave the elites and the people what they wanted and sentenced the man to death. The governor then washed his hands and asked, "*What is truth, anyway?*"

Fast forward 2,000 years.

In any given province of the great American Empire, the political, social and media elites say, "*The truth is . . .*" and the people, believing the lie, repeat it. The facts, it seems, do not matter anymore today than they did 2,000 years ago. The "*truth*" is whatever lie is repeated most fervently. The "*truth*" is whatever lie is repeated the loudest. The "*truth*" is whatever lie is repeated most often.

Are we to wash our hands?

OCTOBER 24, 2016

Many years ago, I had a roommate. I remember asking my roommate, *"Where's the TV remote? I want to watch 'The Crucible."* And his reply, *"I read that book."* A discussion then ensued about the book. I never found that remote and I missed the movie.

Now you know why, when we ask a politician, *"Where's the remote?"* he or she responds, *"I read that book."*

OCTOBER 25, 2016

In the darkness, there are monsters everywhere.

Lying in his bed, the man could see in the distorted shadows of the corner. The monster was sitting there, watching him. He was afraid, and so he pulled the covers up to his neck as if that could protect him and watched the monster, wondering, "*When will it pounce?*" The fear within grew. He knew that the monster was there and that it would devour him. After a time, he could take the fear no more and he quickly got out of bed and turned on the light. In the light, he saw that the "*monster*" in truth was nothing more than the pile of dirty laundry that his wife had lied about when said she had put them in the hamper earlier that evening. He laughed at his foolishness and was annoyed with his wife. He turned off the light and went back to sleep.

A short time later, he awoke to a noise that seemed to emanate from under his bed. He listened intently, but heard it no more. He pulled the covers up to his neck as if that could protect him and then heard the noise again. Wide awake now, he lie silently trying in vain to hear the noise, but it did not manifest. Frightened still, he got up, crossed the room and turned on the light. He peered under the bed, but there was nothing. He sat down on the bed and heard the creaking of the bed springs. In the light, he saw that the *"monster"* in truth, was nothing more than the squeaky bedsprings. The mattress seller had lied when he said that the mattress was silent. He laughed at his foolishness and was rankled with the mattress seller. He turned off the light and went back to sleep.

A short time later, he awoke to a scratching outside his window. *"Now,"* he thought, *"it's nothing. There is no monster outside trying to get in."* Nonetheless, he was frightened and he kept feeling that tingling at the back of his neck. He pulled the covers up to his neck as if that could protect him. Eventually, he got up, grabbed a flashlight and went outside to see what was making the noise. He found a tree in need of pruning and a limb that abutted the window. In the light, he saw that the *"monster"* in truth, was nothing more than this limb. The gardener had lied when he said he had trimmed the tree. He laughed at his foolishness and was agitated with the gardener. He went inside and back to sleep.

A short time later, yet again, he was awakened, this time by the sound of creaking from above his head on the second floor. Surely, these were not footsteps? He was afraid. He pulled the covers up to his neck as if that could protect him. After a time, he went upstairs and turned on the light. There was nothing there. He listened intently and determined that the pipes were old. In the light, he saw that the *"monster"* in truth, was nothing more than the sounds of a un-replaced pipe. The contractor had lied when said he

127

had replaced it. The man was angry with the contractor. He returned to his bed and went back to sleep.

In the morning, he awoke, having had a fretful night of sleep. In the light of the dawn, he was no longer afraid, but when he sat up and saw muddy footprints near his bed his heart jumped to his throat. He followed the footprints that led outside, the foot prints that led under his bed, the footprints that led where his dirty clothing had lain and the footprints that led into the room up the stairs. He followed the footprints everywhere he had thought he heard a monster the night before. But, in the light, he saw that the *"monster"* in truth, was nothing more than his own footprints from the night before. He had lied to himself when said he said he was not afraid and he was furious at himself for the lie.

In the light of truth, we see that the only monster is the one made in the distorted darkness of deceit and in the anger that we feel, but. . .

In that darkness, there are monsters everywhere.

OCTOBER 27, 2016

This creepy clown phenomenon has gotten out of hand!

There are clowns in the woods, clowns in our neighborhoods, clowns in the streets and clowns in the city.

There were a couple of creepy clowns that broke into a house in or near Dallas, Texas and shot some people with a BB gun. There are even reports of these creepy clowns around the US Capitol building and trying to get into the White House. These clowns are frightening to men, women and children. They are stealing our money, our security and our peace of mind. It has to stop!

I have a plan. If we all can come together, on November 8, we can send these creepy clowns packing.

NOVEMBER 2, 2016

The American system of criminal justice is premised, in large part, on the presumption of innocence — i.e. a defendant is innocent of a crime until proven guilty in a court of law.

A smart attorney will ask potential jurors before they are empaneled about their preconceived notions related to the defendant and the offense. The attorney will ask, *"Do you believe the defendant is more likely guilty or innocent?"* Many, in a misguided attempt to be fair minded, will say: *"I don't know, I haven't seen the evidence and can't make up my mind until I do."*

That answer is wrong.

The correct answer is that the defendant is innocent unless and until the state meets its burden to prove that defendant guilty.

It is a shame when we allow our preconceived notions to subvert the presumption of innocence.

Nᴏᴠᴇᴍʙᴇʀ 3 2016

OFFICIAL 2016 PRESIDENTIAL BALLOT

BUFFOON

CROOK

STONER

TREE HUGGER

The baby, whose mind has not yet developed, will have no control over his orifices and will spew his bodily fluids anytime, anywhere.

The adult whose mind has not yet developed will have no control over his mouth and will spew his nonsense anytime, anywhere.

It smells just as bad.

NOVEMBER 5, 2016

In the early 1990s, following a job, I left my home state of Texas and moved to California. This was during the height of the Rush Limbaugh days. He was on the radio, had a TV show and a book out. I had never heard of him, had never heard his radio show, had never seen his television show, and had never read his book. I recall having a conversation with a coworker who adamantly hated Mr. Limbaugh. She told me how he was racist, bigoted, misogynistic, etc.

"Have you ever heard his radio show?" I asked.

"No," she replied, *"I wouldn't listen to that garbage."*

"Have you ever seen his television show?" I asked

"No," she replied, *"I would never watch that man on anything."*

"Have you read his book?" I asked.

"No," she replied, *"I have no interest in anything he has to say."*

I asked: *"Then how do you know he is a racist, bigot or misogynist? You have never heard him speak. You have never watched his television show. You have never read his words."* I certainly could not reach that conclusion without reviewing the body of his work. She got very angry with me. She said that because I am from Texas I was a *"right wing nutcase — everyone from Texas is."* This was, of course, news to me.

In recent years, I have had occasion to discuss with friends the various news outlets.

Some detest one cable news network: *"They are all a bunch of idiotic liberals."*

Some detest another news network: *"They are all a bunch of right wing bigots."*

When I ask: *"Have you watched. . ."* that network

They reply: *"I would never watch. . ."* that network.

And so I ask, *"How can you presume to judge the people on that network, when you say you do not watch it?"*

In recent weeks, I see posts where individuals re-post memes that are factually inaccurate and point to them to justify their beliefs.

When I ask: *"Have you researched the assertions being made?"*

The answer is invariably: *"No."*

And so, I ask,

How can we know another's words, when we refuse to learn what they say?

How can we know another's view, when we refuse to learn what they see?

How can we know another's mind, when we refuse to learn their thoughts?

Again, I ask . . .

How can we know, when we refuse to learn?

November 8, 2016

Those who know me know that I was not a supporter of either Mr. Trump or Ms. Clinton during this election. Nonetheless, the American people have spoken and congratulations are in order to Donald Trump on his victory last night.

In my humble opinion, this was not a rebuke of the Democratic Party or the Democratic Party principles. Nor was this an embrace of the Republican Party or the Republican Party principles.

This was/is a backlash against a political-financial-social-media oligarchy that, for years now, has been telling the American people, *"Shut up. We are smarter and better than you and you should just do what we say."*

But Joe Average had other ideas. Joe Average replied: *"I am tired of politics as usual. I am tired of the oligarchy telling me what I need to do."* He said: *"I am mad as hell and I am not going to take it anymore."* And both of the aforementioned parties comprise the membership of that oligarchy. The American people have spoken. They have sent a warning shot against the bow of the oligarchy. Right or wrong, they have said: "*Ya basta! — Enough, already.*"

Now is the time for each and every one of us to come together as a people, as a nation and in one voice hold Mr. Trump accountable. Mr. Trump, you said that you would drain the swamp. We expect you to do so. And we expect our elected officials to start representing "*we the people*" instead of their own interests. Good luck and God speed.

A child, when not properly raised, will throw a tantrum when he does not get his way. How are we raising our children?

If our psyches are so fragile that we must seek therapy after the results of an election, then we have bigger problems than who will be the next president.

November 11, 2016

We riot 'cuz we do not like,
The things that people say,
We riot and prepare to fight,
All the night and day.

We riot when we win,
We riot when we lose,
We riot and we sin,
We riot when we choose.

We riot for we do not like,
To hear you and your voice,
We riot and say "take a hike,"
We do not like your choice.

Mario Kiefer

"My way or the highway,"
From the street we scream and shout,
"Don't like my way, then there's the door,
Use it and get out."

We riot when we disagree,
With choices that are made,
We riot for we cannot see,
The path that has been laid.

We do not riot for our rights,
Or a future we cannot know,
We riot 'cuz we've lost our sight,
And know not how to grow.

We riot solely out of fear,
Of a future we cannot see,
We riot for we cannot bear,
To let others live out free.

We riot and proclaim that ours,
Is the only math,
How dare we let another man,

Make and choose his path.

We riot when we lose,
We riot when we win,
We riot when we choose,
We riot and we sin.

November 12, 2016

With all of the hullabaloo over the election, I cannot help but think, we've seen this song and dance before.

Does anyone else remember . . .

1980: Ronald Reagan was elected President of the United State and people said:

He is going to lead us into a nuclear WWIII.

He is going to round up homosexuals and minorities into concentration camps.

America is dead! Life as we know it is over.

1992: Bill Clinton was elected President of the United States and people said:

He is going to lead us into a nuclear WWIII.

He is going to round up Christians and conservatives into concentration camps.

America is dead! Life as we know it is over.

2000: George W. Bush was elected President of the United States and people said

He is going to lead us into a nuclear WWIII.

He is going to round up homosexuals and minorities into concentration camps.

America is dead! Life as we know it is over.

2008: Barack Obama was elected President of the United States and people said:

He is going to lead us into a nuclear WWIII.

He is going to round up Christians and conservatives into concentration camps.

America is dead! Life as we know it is over.

2016: Donald Trump was elected President of the United States and people said:

He is going to lead us into a nuclear WWIII.

He is going to round up homosexuals and minorities into concentration camps.

America is dead! Life as we know it is over.

Does anyone else remember? We've seen this song and dance before.

NOVEMBER 12, 2016

Watching the protests over the election, I cannot help but think of this quote:

"The soul of man does violence to itself, first of all, when it becomes an abscess and, as it were, a tumour on the universe, so far as it can. For to be vexed at anything which happens is a separation of ourselves from nature, in some part of which the natures of all other things are contained. In the next place, the soul does violence to itself when it turns away from any man, or even moves towards him with the intention of injuring, such as are the souls of those who are angry. In the third place, the soul does violence to itself when it is overpowered by pleasure or by pain. Fourthly, when it plays a part, and does or says anything insincerely and untruly. Fifthly, when it allows any act of its own and any movement to be without an aim, and does anything thoughtlessly and without considering what it is, it being right that even the smallest things be done with reference to an end; and the end of rational animals is to follow the reason and the law of the most ancient city and polity." ~Marcus Aurelius in his book *Meditations*.

Marcus Aurelius was a Roman emperor from 161 AD to 180 AD. He was the last of what has been called the five good emperors. He worked diligently to solve some of

Rome's pressing problems at the time and was a Stoic philosopher. He wrote in his book *"Meditations"* about his Stoic philosophy. Periodically, I will re-read this book and each time I do, I find something new to take away. It should be mandatory reading in school.

November 13, 2016

I wrote this about a month ago.

"You want tolerance so badly, that you denigrate those who are not tolerant.

You want love so badly, that you hate those who do not love.

"You want justice so badly, that you are willing to commit a crime to get it.

"You want peace so badly, that you are willing to do violence for it.

"Do your actions bring about the goal you seek or in the acting, do you destroy the goal?"

As I wake this morning and watch the news, I think that the underlying questions in that post bear repeating:

If . . . you seek tolerance so badly, then why do you denigrate those with whom you disagree? Or is tolerance only for those who think like you?

If . . . you seek a love that trumps hate, then why do you say such hateful things? Or is love reserved only for those who feel like you?

If . . . you seek justice so badly, then why do you commit crimes? Or is justice reserved only for those who agree with you?

If . . . you seek peace so badly, then why are you willing to be so violent? Or is peace reserved only for those who act like you?

Again, I ask,

Do your actions bring about the goal you seek or in the acting, do you destroy the goal?

NOVEMBER 15, 2016

You are traveling along a mountain road and come across a fork in the path. One fork leads down the mountain and the other leads up. The fork that leads down the mountain is paved, has good drainage and is generally easy to follow. The fork that leads up the mountain is arduous, rocky and difficult to climb.

Which road do you take? The high road or the low road?

NOVEMBER 23, 2016

Pulling out various editions of my Merriam Webster's dictionary, I am trying to find out when the word *"peaceful"* began to include throwing rocks, smashing windows, setting cars and buildings on fire, pulling people from cars and beating them and/or beating people in parking garages. For my own education, I am hoping that someone can help me find where in these various editions of the dictionary the definition includes those examples.

NOVEMBER 24 2016

Happy Thanksgiving!

Today, I want to remember and to give thanks for all those things in my life:

I am thankful for the love and support of good friends and family

I am thankful for a decent job — even it sometimes drives me crazy.

I am thankful for the roof over my head, the clothes on my back and the food in belly.

I am thankful for my health, such that it is.

I am thankful for all the blessings that God has chosen to bestow upon me.

I am thankful for the challenges in life that have taught me to be strong and to appreciate the good things.

I am thankful for the strength to endure the *"slings and arrows of outrageous fortune."*

I am thankful for the love of my spouse.

Let's remember to take time aside today to give thanks for this last year's harvest and remember that, you reap what you sow.

The wrench is a tool used to provide grip and mechanical advantage in applying torque to turn fasteners such as nuts and bolts. The wrench neither knows nor cares how tightly it turns the fastener. It simply acts in accordance with the will of the one wielding it

The screwdriver is a tool for turning screws that the user inserts into the screw head to turn it. The screwdriver neither knows nor cares how deep it goes into the shaft. It simply acts in accordance with the will of the one wielding it.

A hammer is a tool or device that delivers a blow to an object to drive nails, fit parts, forge metal, and break apart objects. The hammer neither knows nor cares how hard the blow. It simply acts in accordance with the will of the one wielding it.

What do you call a man who neither knows nor cares how he is being used, and simply acts in accordance with the will of the one wielding him?

NOVEMBER 26, 2016

I once stood up on a bus and offered my seat to a lady. I was raised to believe it was a kindness to give my seat to another. She proceeded to berate me for being a misogynist. Did I think her incapable of standing? Did I think she was some frail flower that needed a big, powerful man to take care of her? She was perfectly capable of caring for herself! Of course, I apologized. I did not mean to offend.

I once knew a woman who sneezed. My immediate reflex was to say, *"God bless you."* I was raised to believe that it was a kindness to offer support to someone who was ill. This woman became apoplectic. She was so offended by the phrase *"God bless you."* How dare I say that to her! Didn't I know she was an atheist? How dare I assume that she would be pleased by that sentiment. She was so offended. Of course, I apologized. I did not mean to offend.

I once knew a man who lost a loved one. When I heard the news, I told him that my prayers were with him. I was raised to believe that it was a kindness to offer support to those in pain. He became extremely offended. He didn't want or need my prayers. *"God is a myth,"* he said, *"a crutch used by the unenlightened.*" He didn't want my prayers or my comfort. He was so offended by the phrase *"my prayers are with you.*" Of course, I apologized. I did not mean to offend.

Do we truly live in a society where a simple kindness is deemed offensive?

And in the asking, of course, I apologize. I do not mean to offend.

November 27, 2016

Every man must pick and choose,
The path that he will seek.
Every man must pick and choose,
The words that he will speak.

Every man must daily choose,
The actions he will take,
For good or ill, the lot is drawn,
What mark it is he'll make?

The path we tread often finds,
Those with whom we disagree.
Ours the choice not to mind,
Those who will not see.

The choice is yours, be false or true,
And act on this desire,
But remember that for all the while,
You're seen in this attire.

Every man must pick and choose,
The path that he will seek.
Every man must pick and choose,
The words that he will speak.

The US Supreme Court ruled that burning the American flag is a form of free speech protected by the First Amendment to the Constitution. Many people are very offended by this form of speech, but it is protected by the Constitution and cannot be banned.

Yet. . .

The very people who so vociferously defend their right to burn the flag as a form of free speech are so often the same people who want "*safe zones*" on college campuses to protect them from speech that offends them.

It seems that some people believe that they should be protected from offensive speech — but only that speech which offends them.

Oh, the irony!

My generation did an admirable job of teaching our children when to stand up, when to speak out, and to value their own self-worth.

My generation did a terrible job of teaching our children when to sit down, when to shut up, when to listen, and to value the worth of others.

I love stew. A great stew is made when you take only the best ingredients and cook them over low heat in one big pot, slowly letting them simmer together until a rich gravy is made that is seasoned by each. In every bite, one tastes the sumptuousness of each and every ingredient. By melding the separate components together in one pot, we get a rich, delicious, hearty meal that can be enjoyed by everyone.

I enjoy salad. A great salad is made by layering ingredients throughout. It's built upon a bed of lettuce (iceberg or romaine — your choice) with other ingredients added to build flavor; perhaps cherry tomatoes and sliced cucumber; maybe a little grated carrot and sliced mushroom. Throw on some avocado and sliced hard-boiled egg for good measure. Then top with your favorite dressing to bring the ingredients together. Each bite has distinct flavors, but you don't always get everything in one bite. While I enjoy the salad, the meal is just not as hearty and tasty as the stew.

I don't care for a meal where the food is compartmentalized. But some people detest when the protein touches the starch. They don't want their vegetables mixed with the potatoes and they eschew a gravy that covers the entire meal. They complain that the vegetables appropriate the flavor of the protein. When you take a bite from this meal, you enjoy the taste only from the compartment that you sample and miss out on the other flavors being offered. When sampling each ingredient individually and failing to meld together the flavors, the dish seems unfinished and is not very satisfying.

The stew is hardy, rich and flavorful.

The salad is tasty, but not as sumptuous as the stew.

The compartmentalized meal is lacking and unfinished.

When preparing the great American meal, shouldn't we strive to meld the various ingredients of the many cultures that are represented in our society into one rich, sumptuous and delicious stew?

Some people prefer their food compartmentalized. Some people prefer a salad.

Personally, I love the stew.

Dear Santa:

I know that you are very busy and that your elves are making lots of toys for all the good little boys and girls, so, I will (try to) keep this brief.

I have a good life and I need for nothing that I do not have, and the things that I want, I have the means to get. But, I have been a good boy this year and here is what I ask for this Christmas:

For those who are thirsty, send them drink;

For those who are hungry, send them food;

For those who are cold, send them warmth;

For those who are ignorant, send them knowledge;

For those who are cruel, send them kindness;

For those who hate, send them love.

Thank you, and Merry Christmas.

December 11, 2016

I saw a story on the news this morning about a couple who went to a restaurant and were so offended by the music being played (Christmas Carols) that when they left they gave a note to the owner complaining that all of the *"religious themed"* music was *"offensive."* To that couple, I say . . . some people actually enjoy the Christmas season including the Christmas Carols. The only thing that was offensive in what occurred, is your attempt to censor the speech of others.

And it got me to thinking . . .

A Jewish friend of mine once wished me a *Chanukah Sameach*. I said, *"Thank you."*

A Muslim friend of mine once wished me *Ramadan Mubarak*. I said, *"Thank you."*

A Bahai friend once wished me a happy *Naw Ruz*. I said, *"Thank you."*

A Buddhist friend of mine once wished me a happy *Magha Puja*. I said, *"Thank you."*

A Wiccan friend of mine once wished me a happy *Samhain*. I said, *"Thank you."*

A Chinese friend of mine once wished me *Gung Hey Fat Choy*. I said, *"Thank you."*

To all of my friends who send me wishes of good will during the seasons they celebrate, I say, *"Thank you for the good wishes."* I know they come from your heart.

To that couple, and others like them, I say: if you are so insecure in your own beliefs that you are offended when others express theirs; if you are so insecure in your own beliefs that you cannot graciously say *"thank you"* when one wishes you good will; then you have bigger problems than being offended by the music someone plays or by the phrase someone chooses to make the wish of good will.

December 13, 2016

I have been reading the stories about those who were *"traumatized"* by the recent election. Seriously, you are *"traumatized"* by the election results and need an *"emotional service"* animal or some other therapy to get by?

Well, I say, get a grip!

Real trauma is losing your job of thirty years because your employer decides to move operations overseas.

Real trauma is spending tens of thousands of dollars on a useless degree because you wanted something creative and being unable to find a job.

Real trauma is losing your home to fire or flood and living on the streets — through no fault of your own.

Real trauma is watching your crops die from lack of water knowing that you will never be able to make up the loss.

Real trauma is facing down sniper gunfire to protect the others in your squad; or getting your legs blown off by an IED.

Real trauma is the losing a loved one to some terrorist event across the globe.

Real trauma is suffering rape, maiming, torture and death at the hands of criminals run amok.

Real trauma is knowing that you will never walk again because some idiot couldn't put their phone down long enough to pay attention to what they were doing on the road.

Real trauma is watching your friend die because some fool got behind the wheel after one too many cocktails.

Real trauma is holding a loved one in your arms as they succumb to some heinous disease.

If you are so *"traumatized"* by the election results that you need an *"emotional service"* animal or some other therapy, your life has been **way too soft**.

Remember the adage, I thought my life was terrible, because I had no shoes, until I saw the man with no feet.

Count your blessings and get a grip.

Today, I saw a post that accused Donald Trump of having relations with his daughter, Ivanka. To that, I respond:

When I am wrong, I am wrong and I will be the first to admit it. And this is one of those times when I have to admit that I was wrong.

I am not a fan of the President-Elect, but when people said that they were so distraught over the election that they needed to seek therapy, I said, *"Get a grip. The results of an election shouldn't cause you to need therapy."*

But, if your heart is so filled with hate that you are willing to spew this kind of garbage, then I have to admit, I was wrong and you DO need therapy.

DECEMBER 17, 2016

I have done a lot of traveling and each time I go somewhere, I am struck by the number of people at the airport who are heading to the same place as I while dragging their luggage behind them. I wonder, what all have they packed? Why is their luggage so heavy? Since we are headed to the same destination, why do some people bring carts filled with a number of suitcases, while others take only a piece of carry-on?

Each time that we prepare to travel, it is a challenge to decide what to take and what to leave behind and each traveler faces this dilemma — wondering:

Will I need this or that?

Will I regret not bringing this or that?

If we don't bring enough, we won't have what we need when we reach our destination, but if we bring too much, our luggage will be heavy. So, how do we choose?

However you choose, remember that choice on what you pack is yours to make alone. You decide what to take and how heavy your luggage is going to be. And, because the choice on what to pack is yours alone, the burden to carry is also. And only you can decide what burden you can bear.

Some of us have a lot of luggage and a heavy burden, while others have only a carry-on, and a much lighter load. But ultimately, you choose what to pack.

Each time that we prepare to travel, it is a challenge to decide what to take and what to leave behind. You choose, but remember, we are all headed to the same destination.

December 28, 2016

They say that, *"the truth"* will set you free, but that same *"truth"* can also bind.

Often people will shout from the rooftops their judgment, loudly proclaiming, *"I only speak 'the truth'."* But *"the truth"* is a fickle mistress and subject to the perceptions of its proclaimer. That is why, two thousand years ago, Pilate famously asked, *"What is truth?"* and washed his hands. In that simple act, he condemned an innocent man to crucifixion. And, while the Devil has been called many things, chief among them the Prince of Lies, in reality, the Devil never lies. He is the ultimate truth-teller.

Evil flourishes:

When *"the truth"* is only half-told;

When *"the truth"* is told not to enlighten, but to darken the waters;

When *"the truth"* is told not to move others toward a righteous path, but to stir hatred;

When *"the truth"* is told to create contempt;

When "*the truth*" is told for distraction;

When "*the truth*" is told to sow discord and distrust.

Evil flourishes not in the lies that people tell, but in "*the truth*" that is uttered when that "*truth*" is wielded as a weapon to divide and destroy. When used as such, it is not a tool for good, but rather, it is a tool for evil being wielded by the Prince. You see, the Devil has no need for lies, when "*the truth*" can be used toward his aim. Evil flourishes when "*the truth*" is used for ill.

So, before making that proclamation, "*I only speak 'the truth*'" ask yourself, are you being a tool for good or a tool for ill? And take care when speaking "*the truth*," for although. . .

They say that "*the truth*" will set you free, that same "*truth*" can also bind.

JANUARY 10, 2017

I detest bagging my own groceries. I also detest waiting because the person in front of me will not do their own. Alas, this is just another of those niceties of life that have gone the wayside.

Remember when:

Razor blades and cold medicine were not locked up?

Gas stations had full service; they pumped your gas, washed your windshield and checked your fluids (and tire pressure)?

The grocery stores not only bagged the groceries, but carried them to the car for you?

The store clerk actually counted your change to you, so that you knew you were getting the correct change?

Store clerks smiled and told you how much you were to pay, and said *"please," "thank you,"* and *"come again"* instead of just pointing to the register so that you could read the amount being charged?

We have become so addicted to expedience and convenience that we have let all those little things that make the experience pleasant fall away.

The real question, in my mind, is not why someone would not bag their own groceries, but why the grocery store does not have enough staff to make the shopping experience more pleasant. The store that gets my business is not the store that makes everything expedient, but rather the store that makes me feel that they are happy I am there.

Mario Kiefer

JANUARY 10, 2017

Nothing ever changes, but the names and the places.

JANUARY 11, 2017

Remember when . . . innuendo and rumor were published in the gossip pages?

Today . . . we call it *"unsourced"* or *"unverified"* news reports and splash it on the front page.

I wonder if Edward Murrow would be proud.

January 12, 2017

I am a simple man with simple thoughts and simple ideas. I believe in balance in thought, word and deed.

I am a simple man with simple thoughts and simple ideas. I believe in the principles that have made this nation great; that people can and should have the freedom of political ideology and the free expression thereof.

I am a simple man with simple thoughts and simple ideas. I believe that no man, no group, no organization is 100% evil or 100% good. Each, and every one of us, has his virtue and his vice.

I am a simple man with simple thoughts and simple ideas. I believe that no ideology is 100% correct or 100% wrong. Each has its good points and bad.

I am a simple man with simple thoughts and simple ideas. I believe that we must come up with a balanced approach to the myriad problems that we face by implementing the good ideas and discarding the bad ones. It should not matter whence that idea comes.

I am a simple man with simple thoughts and simple ideas. I believe that it is sad, but true, that in this hyper-politicized, hyper-polarized society that is so prone to hyperbolic rhetoric where too many of us say, *"Either you are with us or you are against us and if you are against us you are evil,"* it seems that there is no room for fair-minded thinking. It seems that there is no room for a balanced approach. So, it becomes difficult to have a fair-minded and reasonable conversation with those who are so unwilling to even discuss an opposing point of view.

I am a simple man with simple thoughts and simple ideas, and I believe that it is impossible to have a balanced approach when dealing with those who are unbalanced.

January 12, 2017

There is a controversy on Capitol Hill related to a certain piece of art that is hanging in the Capitol building. Some people find the artwork distasteful and offensive and have been taking it down. Others claim that the artwork is an expression of political thought that should not be censored and should be hung in the Capitol to depict the experiences of a segment of the population.

I am no art critic and generally have no opinion on art. My only question is this (and I ask, because I honestly do not know the answer): how much taxpayer money is being spent on art to hang in the Capitol?

Perhaps Congress should purchase its art, if they must purchase it at all, from a discount retailer. It would not offend anyone and would likely cost a lot less.

JANUARY 13, 2017

Sometimes, it is better to allow a display of ignorance to speak for itself.

JANUARY 15, 2017

A pun, just for fun:

I used to know these two people. One was named John and the other Mary. John and I were friends and, because we were friends, I often teased and cajoled John. Mary was an acquaintance that I did not particularly care for, and because I did not like her, I would never tease Mary.

One day, John asked me, *"Why are you always picking on me? You never pick on Mary."*

I told John, *"I pick on you because I like you. You are pick-able. I don't pick on Mary because I don't like her. She is dis-pick-able."*

JANUARY 21, 2017

As I was driving in my car yesterday, I listened to the many speeches being made during the inauguration of our 45th president. As I listened to the news and events occurring yesterday and again this morning, I was both inspired and saddened.

In 1789, George Washington gave the very first presidential inaugural address. He concluded his speech saying that the ". . . *Parent of the Human Race . . . has been pleased to favor the American people with opportunities for deliberating in perfect tranquility, and dispositions for deciding with unparalleled unanimity on a form of government for the security of their union and the advancement of their happiness.*"

Washington was extolling the virtue of our ability to choose our government and its form. He expressed that government derives its authority from the consent and unity of the people. Before this time, governments were changed most often at the tip of a spear or sword. America was (and is) unique among the nations of the world, in that every four years we go through this exercise where we celebrate the peaceful transition of power from one "*king*" to another. I am inspired by our long history of such peaceful transition.

But then, I am saddened.

As I watch and listen to events unfold — the violent protests in the street and the divisions we continue to foster. I feel a foreboding as I recall the words of Sun Tzu, who, in the sixth century before Christ, wrote in *The Art of War* that: "*If sovereign and subject are in accord, put division between them.*" He spoke of dividing a people against their government and against themselves in order to defeat them.

And then, I am reminded, that in the gospels of Matthew and Luke, Jesus said, "*. . . If a kingdom is divided against itself, it cannot stand. If a house is divided against itself, it cannot stand . . .*" and how Abraham Lincoln famously echoed these words when, in 1858, at the Illinois Republican State Convention, he was chosen as the Republican candidate for US Senate and said that, "*[a] house divided against itself cannot stand . . .*" Lincoln of course was speaking of the division in our nation over slavery and economic systems that derived their treasure from that slave labor. But he also was speaking of division in community.

Today, we divide ourselves in any number of ways: by race, creed, color, national origin, gender, or gender orientation. We divide ourselves by political party, economic class, and political ideology. We have forgotten how to be united.

Eleanor Roosevelt famously said: "*Pit race against race, religion against religion, prejudice against prejudice. Divide and conquer! We must not let that happen here.*" She was right. And yet, we let it happen.

And as I watch the violence, the hateful rhetoric being hurled by both sides against *"the other"*, I recall the words of T.H. White in *The Once and Future King* when he wrote that, *"The Destiny of Man is to unite, not to divide. If you keep on dividing you end up as a collection of monkeys throwing nuts at each other out of separate trees."*

And I am saddened because, if a house divided cannot stand, I wonder whether the more appropriate question is, should it? For if we continue down the path of division, surely we will be no more than that collection of monkeys.

JANUARY 21, 2017

A certain celebrity tweeted a call for the military to step in to prevent Donald Trump from taking office.

According to <u>18 USC 2385 - Advocating the overthrow of Government,</u>

"*Whoever knowingly or willfully advocates, abets, advises, or teaches the duty, necessity, desirability, or propriety of overthrowing or destroying the government of the United States or the government of any State, Territory, District or Possession thereof, or the government of any political subdivision therein, by force or violence, or by the assassination of any officer of any such government; or*

Whoever, with intent to cause the overthrow or destruction of any such government, prints, publishes, edits, issues, circulates, sells, distributes, or publicly displays any written or printed matter advocating, advising, or teaching the duty, necessity, desirability, or propriety of overthrowing or destroying any government in the United States by force or violence, or attempts to do so; or

Whoever organizes or helps or attempts to organize any society, group, or assembly of persons who teach, advocate, or encourage the overthrow or destruction of any such government by force or violence; or becomes or is a member of, or affiliates with, any such society, group, or assembly of persons, knowing the purposes thereof--

Shall be fined under this title or imprisoned not more than twenty years, or both, and shall be ineligible for employment by the United States or any department or agency thereof, for the five years next following his conviction.

If two or more persons conspire to commit any offense named in this section, each shall be fined under this title or imprisoned not more than twenty years, or both, and shall be ineligible for employment by the United States or any department or agency thereof, for the five years next following his conviction.

As used in this section, the terms "organizes" and "organize", with respect to any society, group, or assembly of persons, include the recruiting of new members, the forming of new units, and the regrouping or expansion of existing clubs, classes, and other units of such society, group, or assembly of persons."

(June 25, 1948, ch. 645, 62 Stat. 808; July 24, 1956, ch. 678, § 2, 70 Stat. 623; Pub. L. 87–486, June 19, 1962, 76 Stat. 103; Pub. L. 103–322, title XXXIII, § 330016(1)(N), Sept. 13, 1994, 108 Stat. 2148.)

JANUARY 25, 2017

It is simple really. If you want respect, you must be respectable.

Some college campuses are having riots as so-called protesters attempt to prevent conservatives from speaking. I cannot help but wonder, if we are not allowed to hear another speak, how can we judge whether what that person says is odious?

Those who engage in the destruction of property, engage in odious acts. Are we to take the word of those who do so that what another says is evil?

Are we not allowed to hear and judge for ourselves?

February 3, 2017

More riots on campus.

Let's be clear these are not protesters. They are not advocating for or against any particular economic, social or political cause. They are not seeking a redress of grievances. They're not trying to bring awareness to an issue.

These are thugs, sociopaths and psychopaths. Their sole intention is to engage in violent acts. Sure, they mask their activities by using socially acceptable words and a pretended alignment against bigotry, racism, and sexism. But in truth, when they act out against a speaker, it matters not who is speaking or what the topic is. They use the speaker or topic as an excuse to engage in the violence that brings them a perverse pleasure.

We must recognize these individuals for what they are: individuals in dire need of mental health treatment to discover the root cause as to why they get their perverse pleasure from pain. Then we must provide them with the treatment that they need in order to learn empathy, and how to channel their feelings in a constructive manner. Perhaps commitment to a psyche ward until they can show that they are no longer a danger to themselves or others is warranted.

But until we recognize that they are not protesters, but rather roving bands of sick individuals, we will never be able to help them. Step one is recognizing the problem and calling it by its proper name.

In the 1970s, we taught our children that, "*Sticks and stones may break my bones, but words can never hurt me.*"

In 2017, we teach our children that some words are so hateful, that nobody should hear them. We have told our children that they are entitled to a "*safe space*" free from such horrific micro-aggressions. We have taught our children that they should take whatever steps are necessary to secure this "*safe space.*" We have taught our children that some words, hurt more than sticks and stones.

So, those college students who feel aggrieved by words that constitute such "*micro-aggression*s" should feel free to destroy property, burn cars and physically assault another who says something "*hurtful.*" How else can they secure a "*safe space*" where their fragile egos are not harmed? We teach them that violent acts can (and should) be used against violent speech.

I cannot be the only one that sees the irony.

FEBRUARY 15, 2017

Two thousand years from now, an archaeologist will be digging through the ruins of Washington, DC and come across a treasure trove of the minds we lost in 2016 and 2017.

I read your post and I get your point.

Your point is . . .

. . . You don't like Trump or you don't like Clinton.

. . . You don't like Republicans or you don't like Democrats.

. . . You are for or against gay marriage.

. . . You don't like the travel ban or you do like the travel ban.

. . . You don't like this political ideology or that one.

. . . You think those who disagree with you, are "*MOFOs*" or "*idiots*."

But I don't care about any of that. However,

. . . I do care if you try and do the right thing.

. . . I do care if you show kindness to those who are in pain.

. . . I do care if you are generous to those in need.

. . . I do care if you move toward another to heal or to harm.

. . . I do care if you move with consideration of others.

. . . I do care if you call people names out of spite or anger.

The rest . . . pointless.

Oligarchy (from Greek ὀλιγαρχία [oligarkhía]; from ὀλίγος [olígos], meaning "few", and ἄρχω [arkho], meaning "*to rule or to command*") is a form of power structure in which power rests with a small number of people. These people might be distinguished by nobility, wealth, family ties, education or corporate, religious or military control. Such states are often controlled by a few prominent families who typically pass their influence from one generation to the next, but inheritance is not a necessary condition for the application of this term.

Just think about it.

I saw this post today being spread by someone on social media. It reports to be about the Supreme Court considering removing Donald Trump from the presidency. Posts like these make me wonder about our educational system. I could not believe that people might spread and believe this to be true. I had to respond:

I do not know whether there is a lawsuit out there or not, but it does not matter. The Supreme Court does not have the authority to remove any sitting president.

Under the Constitution, the only way a President can be removed from office (other than resignation, disability or death) is by impeachment followed by a trial in the Senate. The House votes on a bill of impeachment — basically, that is an indictment, then that impeachment is referred to the Senate which holds a trial on the impeachment and decides whether or not to remove the President from office.

Only two US Presidents have been impeached by the House of Representatives — Andrew Johnson in 1868 and Bill Clinton in 1998 — both later acquitted at trials held by the Senate.

The Supreme Court, if it follows the Constitution, cannot remove a sitting president from office. Should the Supreme Court attempt to remove him from office, then they would not be following the Constitution — the very document that they are entrusted to interpret.

Do they no longer read or teach the Constitution in high school?

February 25, 2017

The right believes that one should urinate only in the bathroom of the gender of their birth. If they think that passing such bathroom laws is going to win them elections, they are sadly mistaken.

The left believes that one should urinate in the bathroom of the gender with which they identify. If they think that passing such bathroom laws is going to win them elections, they are sadly mistaken.

I think that I speak for the vast majority of Americans who don't give a flying f$# where one pees as long as they don't miss the toilet.

February 25, 2017

Throughout history, mankind has debated great philosophical thoughts . . .

Which faith is the correct one? Christianity, Judaism, Islam or another?

Which political system is best? Democracy, Monarchy, Communism?

Which economic system is best? Capitalism? Socialism?

Is slavery ever acceptable?

Great minds have argued and debated. Wars have been fought over these weighty issues.

Today, we argue about . . . where to go pee.

To my friends on the left, I say this with love, open your eyes!

You are dismayed and surprised by the Trump victory last November. You ask, "*Why?*" and "*How could this have happened?*"

Well, before the election . . .

. . . Because he supports the police and did not support Black Lives Matter, you called my father a racist. Who do you think he voted for?

. . . Because she is against illegal immigration, you called my sister a bigot. Who do you think she voted for?

. . . Because she is against abortion, you called my friend a misogynist. Who do you think she voted for?

. . . Because he voted for a Republican in a local election, you called my friend an idiot. Who do you think he voted for?

. . . Because she disagreed with your opinions on any one of myriad issues, you called my friend stupid. Who do you think she voted for?

. . . Because my friend supported Donald Trump, you called him a *"mofo."*

Calling people names does not enamor them to your cause. Bullying people who disagree with you, does not make them suddenly agree. These tactics only harden hearts and cause people to act in opposition to you. Do you not see that?

Do you ever wonder how many people supported Trump over your candidate **because** they were tired of being called a racist, bigot, misogynist, idiot, stupid or mofo? Do you ask yourself how many more people you alienate and push into his camp when you persist with calling them names?

You are dismayed and surprised by the Trump victory last November. You ask, *"Why?"* and *"How could this have happened?"* Well, the answer is in front of you if you only look in the mirror.

You are the reason he won.

American Politics: It doesn't matter if you're right or wrong, it only matters what side you're on.

I saw a post and comments thereon alternately decrying or praising Disney's decision to include a gay/questioning character in the new *Beauty and the Beast*. Some have called for a boycott of Disney.

I could be wrong here (I often am.) But I thought the moral lesson in this story was not to judge a book by its cover. I thought the story was meant to teach children that, although someone may appear to be a "*beast*" on the outside, if one looks within, that "*beast*" may actually have a good heart that is filled with love and kindness; and that by showing love and kindness to the "*beast*" one could draw out the beauty within.

Maybe the inclusion of a gay character is to teach people to look to the character's heart — maybe not. I don't know. But, the issue, in my mind, is not whether the character is gay or straight, but rather, does the inclusion of the character advance that moral lesson?

If it does, by all means, include the character. If it does not, then it is irrelevant.

As a disabled, gay, male, over forty, who is half white and half latino, I often have to be VERY careful not to offend myself.

A magician uses his assistant to distract the audience all the while using sleight of hand to make something disappear. And the audience, even knowing they have been tricked, still erupts in applause.

A politician uses the media to distract the public all the while using sleight of hand to make something disappear. And the public, even knowing they have been tricked, erupts in applause.

March 6, 2017

Donald Trump (R) made lewd comments about women to Billy Bush during the presidential campaign. The Right defended him and the Left was outraged.

Cedric Richmond (D) made lewd comments about a particular woman sitting on the sofa in the oval office. The Left defended him and the Right was outraged.

When outrage is selective it is hypocrisy — regardless whether there is an (R) or a (D) after the name.

Which leads me back to something I said the other day:

It doesn't matter if you're right or wrong, it only matters what side you're on.

Dear Businesses:

Just something for you to think about:

The Tale of Two Businesses:

A man walked into the business. He wanted to purchase an item. The item cost $50. As he waited for the sales staff to assist him, he noted that there were staff members on their phones. They were emailing, texting, talking with family/friends, surfing the internet or whatever. He asked one of them to assist him. The staff member rolled her eyes and said, *"Just a minute."* When the staff finally assisted the man, she rang up the item and pointed at the register so that the man would see the price. She did this without saying a word. The man left the item on the counter and walked out of the store — without a word.

The man drove twenty minutes down the road and walked into a competing business. The same item cost $100 at this store. When he walked in, the sales staff promptly and courteously greeted him with *"Good morning, can I help you find something?"* He told the staff member what he was looking for and the staff member walked him to the aisle and helped him choose the item. The staff member asked him if he needed anything else and suggested companion items. The man said, "*No*" and the staff member rang up the item, then said, "*That's $108.*" (After taxes of course.) The man handed the staff member a $100 bill and a $20 bill. The staff member placed the two bills on the register, opened the cash drawer and carefully counted the change.

Handing him $2.00, the staff member said, "*That's $110*," then handed him a $10 bill saying, "*That's $120.*" After the man pocketed his change, the staff member put the cash in the drawer and, as the man was leaving said, "*Thank you, have a great day.*"

From that day forward, the man never visited the first business. Instead, he always drove 20 minutes out of his way to the second business and paid twice as much for the product, but he was happy to do so.

Fast forward three years later. The first business has closed. The second business is thriving.

The quickest way for a business to lose customers is to provide poor customer service.

March 16, 2017

About ten years ago, while I was living in San Francisco, I went to the movie theater. My relationship was new and my partner and I had gone to see the latest movie — I forget what the movie was, but that's not the point of the story.

I will never forget this particular experience. The theater was in Daly City; a suburb of San Francisco. We drove to the cinema, parked in the garage, stood in line and purchased our tickets. We got some popcorn and a couple of sodas, then made our way into the theater. It was very crowded, but we managed to find a couple of seats next to each other down in front, off to the right side, and settled in to enjoy the movie.

While we waited for the movie to start, we watched as more and more people poured into the theater looking for seats and unable to find them, because all of the seats were taken. Obviously, people who had been there watching other movies were sneaking in to see this one. Twice, I even saw someone go down to the exit door and open it up to let others come in who, clearly, had not paid to see any movie — let alone this one.

I nudged my partner and said, *"Look at those kids sneaking in."*

He was angry and wanted to go to management.

I told him, *"Management doesn't care. They've got your money. If they cared they would stop it."*

By this time, there were people standing in the aisles, sitting on the stairs and/or just milling about. Well, I guess somebody complained, because a few minutes thereafter, the manager came into the theater and announced that they had more people in the theater than tickets that had been sold. In the next ten minutes, he said, they would ask to see each patron's ticket stub, and if one did not have a stub, he would be asked to leave the theater, banned from ever coming back and, if necessary, arrested and prosecuted. So, if one did not have a ticket, he had ten minutes to leave.

About half of the theatergoers (presumably the ticket holders) cheered. About half of the theatergoers booed. Nonetheless, a significant number of people left the theater. Then the management came around and checked the ticket stubs of those who remained. All of this, of course, delayed the start of the movie, but when it was done, the theater had only those of us who had stood in line and paid for our tickets. There were a number of empty seats available for those who wanted to purchase a ticket at this time, and my partner and I were able to enjoy the movie in comfort.

It struck me that, if in every theater, management enforced the rules and ensured that only those with tickets were allowed in, then everyone who had followed proper channels to get their tickets could enjoy the movie.

And it made me wonder about the people booing. Did they believe that anyone should be able to see the movie for free?

Today, I wonder whether anyone filed a lawsuit claiming that since they were already in the theater (without a ticket), that mere fact that they were in the theater somehow conveyed upon them the right to stay and watch the movie. And what scares me, is the thought of how many people may have stood outside the theater protesting the actions of management.

The art of compromise is sending each side of the argument away from the table when neither side is happy with the result, but each side can live with it.

March 17, 2017

The man was trying to move a boulder that was blocking a road.

First, he tried brute force. He pushed; he tugged; he pulled; but, try as he might, he was unable to move the boulder.

Next he grabbed a plank of wood, but no matter how hard he pushed with the plank, he was still unable to move the boulder.

Then, he grabbed a block of wood, but again, no matter how hard he pushed with the block, he was still unable to move the boulder.

Finally, he got the bright idea to use the block of wood as a fulcrum and the plank of wood as a lever and by doing so, he was able to move the boulder from the road.

The man could not do it on his own.

The plank of wood could not do it on its own.

The block of wood could not do it on its own.

The parts lacked the necessary strength to accomplish the goal. But when the parts were put together as one whole, the goal was accomplished.

Maybe, if we could see ourselves as one people instead of disparate groups, we could learn to work together and find that the whole is greater than the sum of its parts.

Just a thought.

It seems to me that there is a grave misunderstanding in our society about what our rights are — and what they are not:

We do not have the right to THINGS. For example,

- we do not have the right to a house;

- we do not have the right to a car;

- we do not have the right to a new dress;

- we do not have the right to a television;

- we do not have the right to a cell phone.

We do not have the right to the SERVICES of other people (except where specifically conferred upon us by the Constitution of the United States) for example,

- we do not have the right to the services of a contractor;

- we do not have the right to the services of a mechanic;

- we do not have the right to the services of seamstress or stylist;

- we do not have the right to the services of a cable company;

- we do not have the right to the services of a phone company or internet service provider.

Our rights are not to THINGS or to SERVICES *per se*.

The rights that we have are the ones that allow us to engage in certain actions or to be free from compulsion in others.

We DO have the right to purchase a home, a car, a new dress, television or cell phone.

We DO have the right to purchase services from a contractor, mechanic, seamstress or stylist, cable company, or phone company.

Obtaining and paying for these things and services is our own responsibility.

We do not have the right to things or to services. We do have the right to pursue them of our own accord.

It is our choice to have or have not these things and services. It is our responsibility to obtain them and/or pay for them ourselves.

There are laws, rules and regulations on the books related to the possession, distribution and use of marijuana. Some disagree with those laws, rules and regulations, so they refuse to follow them. Some states have even gone so far as to openly defy these laws, rules and regulations. Those who do not like them need not follow them. The law be damned.

There are laws, rules and regulations on the books related to immigration. Some disagree with those laws, rules and regulations, so they refuse to follow them. Some local governments have even gone so far as to openly defy these laws, rules and regulations. Those who do not like them need not follow them. The law be damned.

There are laws, rules and regulations on the books related to transgender use of bathrooms. Some disagree with those laws, rules and regulations, so they refuse to follow them. Some state and local governments have even gone so far as to openly defy these laws, rules and regulations. Those who do not like them need not follow them. The law be damned.

There are laws, rules and regulations on the books related to discrimination. Some people disagree with those laws, rules and regulations. So, following the logic above, I guess that if one does not like those laws, he need not follow them. The law be damned.

There are those who call for stricter gun control laws. Some disagree with these laws, rules and regulations. I guess, if one disagrees with them, he need not follow them. The law be damned.

Of course, it seems to me that:

American democracy is premised on some simple tenets:

1. The process by which decisions are made will be fair, with participation from all stakeholders; and,

2. That as a society we agree to participate in the process; and,

3. There is no guarantee that we will agree with the result, but we all agree to abide by it.

Increasingly, however, it seems, that when we disagree with the results of the process, we feel free to not follow the result.

Democracy be damned.

MARCH 30, 2017

We are all so a quick to judge.

I remember, years ago, living in San Francisco. As I started down the stairs to the Montgomery Street BART station, I was approached by a homeless person who asked me for a dollar. I said, *"Sorry, I don't have any cash."* He proceeded to berate me.

"Look at you," he said, *"in your fancy suit carrying your fancy briefcase — and you can't even spare one dollar for a man who is homeless and hungry."*

At that time, I did not have a job and had no cash whatsoever. In fact, I was down to the last fifty dollars in my bank account and was uncertain how I would pay my rent the next month. Since, I had just been on a job interview, I was wearing a suit and tie. I was carrying a leather bag that held my resume and other items, something that I had purchased back while I was employed and flush with cash.

I saw this video posted online and heard the man talking to a woman who is taking the money he offers and commenting on her fancy bags. I cannot help but think . . . you don't really know their circumstances.

Before you judge, realize, you may not have all of the facts.

APRIL 11, 2017

So, according to some social media posts, one Congressman is suing about a piece of artwork (mentioned in one of my prior posts). Seriously? The backlog of cases pending before both federal and state courts is astounding. As a result, it can sometimes take years for a case to go to trial.

I cannot be the only one who thinks that the courts have better things to do than rule on these types of petty squabbles. Have we really gotten to a place where even the pettiest of squabbles require judicial intervention? Are we so mired in our own biases that we cannot even come together for a common solution on something as ridiculous as what art to hang on the wall?

APRIL 19, 2017

I received an email this morning indicating that my credit card had been charged for the six month auto-renewal on a water filter. No indication when or if the product would be shipped.

The email said for questions, go to their website . . . I clicked the link to their website and signed into my account. No indication on my account about when the part would be shipped. For questions, it said to click "chat," "email" or call their 1-800 number.

I clicked chat. Clearly, the automated computer chat did not understand my question and suggested I call the phone number.

I called the phone number and was placed in phone tree hell. (Whoever came up with the idea of the phone tree should be drawn and quartered!) After ten minutes on the line, I was finally, directed to a live person. I gave that person my information and question. That person, directed me to a second phone number (nowhere on their website). I called the second phone number and was connected to . . . you guessed it, phone tree hell.

After ten minutes on the second phone line, I finally was directed to a live person. I gave that person my information and question. That person, directed me back to the first phone number. I explained, I had already called that number and was directed to them. They transferred me to a third phone number which put me into — that's right, phone tree hell. After ten minutes on that line, I finally was directed to a live person. I gave that person my information and question.

Forty minutes on email, chat, website and the phone before I finally got the answer to my question.

What was my question: When is the part that should automatically be shipped going to be shipped?

One email,

One chat session,

Three different phone numbers,

Four different people,

All to get the answer to . . .

One question.

When will businesses learn how to provide good customer service?

May 4, 2017

"*Newhart*" was a television show that aired between 1982 through 1990. One of its characters (played by Julia Duffy) was named Stephanie Vanderkellen. Stephanie was a spoiled rich girl who had fallen on hard times and as a consequence worked as a maid in the bed and breakfast that was run by the character played by Bob Newhart.

Throughout the years on the show, whenever Stephanie got into trouble, she would say, in a sing-song voice "*sorry, sorry, sorry*" but always without sincere regret. She knew that the word "*sorry*" would get her out of trouble, even though, she felt no regret for what she had done. Her "*sorry*" had no meaning and therefore no worth.

I will never forget one particular episode however, when the handyman (played by Tom Poston) refused to accept her apology.

"*Does this mean you will stop doing things for me?*" she asked.

And he replied, "*No, I will still do things for you, but we are no longer friends.*"

"*Does this mean you will treat me differently?*" she asked.

"*No*," he replied, "*but we are no longer friends.*"

Although there was no outward change in their interactions, the fact that they "*were no longer friends*" bothered her to no end. Until finally, she understood that what she had done was egregiously offensive to the handyman. Then, and only then, did she understand and regret her actions. It was at that point that she said to him, "*I am sorry*" and truly meant it.

It seems that at least once a week, I read or see some celebrity or politician apologizing for something they said or did knowing that the American people (a rather forgiving lot if ever there was one) would accept their apology. But . . . how rare it is that their apology is said with true remorse and meaning.

It strikes me that, if an apology is meaningless, it is also worthless.

The defunct empire is almost always at its strongest before its fall.

MAY 6, 2017

I wake each morning and ask myself, where has the time gone? Then I look in the mirror and say, "*Oh, there it is.*"

May 10, 2017

Politicians (regardless of political stripe) wonder why? Why has the American public lost faith in its leaders?

Last summer, the FBI Director announced that there was insufficient evidence in the e-mail scandal to pursue criminal charges against the Democratic nominee for president. Most Democrats lauded that decision, while most Republicans scorned it.

In October, the same FBI Director announced that he was reopening that investigation into the e-mail scandal to review new evidence. Most Republicans lauded that decision, while most Democrats scorned it.

Since the election, politicians on each side of the aisle have called for that FBI Director's resignation saying that he has lost the support of the rank and file and could no longer be effective.

Yesterday, the President fired the FBI Director saying that he has lost the support of the rank and file and could no longer be effective.

The very people who, just a few short weeks or months ago, called for the FBI Director's resignation, now decry his termination.

And the American public shakes their collective heads in dismay.

Politicians (regardless of political stripe) wonder why? Why has the American public lost faith in its leaders?

Perhaps, it's because most politicians (regardless of political stripe) are faithless.

Definition of hysteria

1 a psychoneurosis marked by emotional excitability and disturbances of the psychogenic, sensory, vasomotor, and visceral functions

2 a behavior exhibiting overwhelming or unmanageable fear or emotional excess.

For example, the plague had caused mass hysteria in the village.

Just think about it.

I am saddened to read some comments about people who have recently passed.

There is a reason we are not supposed to speak ill of the dead. That reason is that no man lives his life entirely alone. Each and every one of us has someone, somewhere that loves us; whether they be a wife, a child, family or friend. Upon our death, that person will mourn.

It does not matter how we perceive the deceased. It only matters how we treat those who are left behind. Will we be kind to those in mourning? Or will we be cruel?

John Donne probably said it best when he wrote:

"No man is an island entire of itself; every man

is a piece of the continent, a part of the main;

if a clod be washed away by the sea, Europe

is the less, as well as if a promontory were, as

well as any manner of thy friends or of thine

own were; any man's death diminishes me,

because I am involved in mankind.

And therefore never send to know for whom the bell tolls;

it tolls for thee." ~ John Donne, *Devotions upon Emergent Occasions, Meditation XVII*

There is a reason we are not supposed to speak ill of the dead — after all, no man is an island. To all those that have lost someone, I send my prayers and condolences.

I can only hope that on the day of my passing, people will be as kind to those I leave behind.

Sometimes, when I feel like complaining, I am reminded of an old episode of *The Facts of Life*.

Blair Warner (the spoiled rich girl) was complaining to Jo (the girl from the mean streets on the wrong side of the tracks) that she too had problems. She said, *"I have had my share of disappointments — like the time Daddy bought me the brown pony when I wanted the gray one!"*

I am just another spoiled brat, here.

MAY 19, 2017

I could be wrong here, but. . .

In the 1980s, the federal government determined that the drinking age should be twenty-one in all fifty states. To accomplish this goal, they ordered that highway funds would be withheld from any state that refused to raise the legal drinking age. Today, the drinking age is twenty-one in all US jurisdictions. At the time, there were those who argued that the federal government had, not only the right, but the obligation, to withhold funds in an attempt to enforce the law.

I wonder . . .

If a state decided that it did not like the federal laws, rules and regulations as they pertain to non-discrimination and, if that state decided to refuse to enforce those laws, what people would say about withholding federal funds from that state? I suspect that most people would support the federal government's right to withhold those funds . . . but I could be wrong.

If a city in a state decided that it did not like the assault weapons ban and told its residents not to worry about that federal law because the city would not enforce it and would actively work to thwart it, what people would say about withholding federal funds from that city? I suspect that most people would support the federal government's right to withhold those funds . . . but I could be wrong.

If a city in a state decided that it did not like federal immigration law and told its residents not to worry about that federal law because the city would not enforce it and would actively work to thwart it, what people would say about withholding federal funds from that city? I suspect that, like before, most people would support the federal government's right to withhold those funds . . . but I could be wrong.

What sets our nation aside from so many others is that we are a nation of laws that are applicable to each and every one of us. It seems to me that selective enforcement of laws makes us no different from any other banana republic . . . but I could be wrong.

MAY 19, 2017

In the 1990s, the Taliban took over the country of Afghanistan. Immediately, they began destroying and dismantling works of art and statues that had been erected to pagan gods. These works of art offended their current religious sensibilities.

In the 2010s, ISIS has been dismantling and destroying ancient works in places like the City of Palmyra because these works offend their current religious sensibilities.

The United States has joined the world in roundly condemning these acts by the Taliban and ISIS. *"These works of art are part of history and should be maintained,"* we proclaim. *"You cannot judge figures of the past by current social mores. After all, those who do not remember the past are doomed to repeat it."*

Yet, today, in varying jurisdictions across this country, we in the United States, are dismantling and destroying works of art and statues that offend our current political sensibilities.

Who says: *"These works of art are part of history and should be maintained. You cannot judge figures of the past by current social* mores. *After all, those who do not remember the past are doomed to repeat it"*?

Are we doomed to repeat?

MAY 20, 2017

A snowflake is a delicate thing that easily melts upon the touch. But put enough of them together, along with a blowing wind, and they can paralyze a city.

MAY 23, 2017

The lessons we teach our children:

There was no doubt about it; the man was evil — deserving of the death penalty. The man had no compassion for his victim, no kindness for those around him. And when the jury returned the verdict, the courtroom erupted in applause.

On the day he was laid to rest, crowds gathered outside the gates of the cemetery; rejoicing in his death. *"Justice!"* they cried.

I stood nearby the man's gravesite as they lowered his body into his final resting place and watched the very small gathering of mourners.

I looked to the man's mother and saw the stony face of anguish. Here was a woman who knew of the evils her son had perpetrated, but still mourned the loss of her child.

I looked to the man's wife and saw the silent tears that rolled down her cheek. Here was a woman who knew the man was bad, but who still mourned the loss of a husband.

I looked at the face of his child; an eight year old boy who would never understand what evil his father had committed; an eight year old boy who did not care. All the child knew was that his father was gone — he had a daddy no more.

And as I listened to the rejoicing outside the cemetery gates, I wondered:

What lesson are we teaching this child who now is in pain? Are we teaching him to be compassionate and kind, or are we teaching the child to be cruel and heartless — as cruel and heartless as those who had no compassion for the grieving family? As cruel and heartless as the man himself?

And I wondered, in twenty years, what kind of man will that eight year child become with the lessons that we teach him?

May 23, 2017

The nucleus of an atom is, in part, made of protons and neutrons. It has a strong nuclear force that holds the protons and neutrons together. The nucleus balances the forces of the protons and neutrons. If the ratio of protons to neutrons is poor, then the atom becomes unstable and decays, emitting radiation in the process.

Some atoms are on the precipice having just enough force to hold the atom's constituent parts together, and any small change in this delicate balance can throw the ratio off, causing nuclear fission. That fission, or splitting apart, emits a great deal of energy and, if uncontrolled, acts upon other atoms causing a nuclear explosion.

Society is like that atom. It is made of parts that are held together by the nucleus of its ideals. Some societies are on the precipice having just enough of the nuclear force to hold it together. When the ratio becomes unmanageable, the force that holds the society together becomes fissile.

What happens to the society when the nucleus breaks apart?

Reflections of a time long gone,

How quickly it has passed.

Present strife, the question begs,

Is nothing meant to last?

JUNE 4, 2017

Things my mama used to say:

"Don't tell me <u>why</u> it <u>can't</u> be done. Tell me <u>how</u> it <u>can</u>."

June 5, 2017

Too many fault lines:

One of my favorite plays is Sondheim's *Into the Woods*. The play is a melding of various fairy tales into one (Cinderella, Little Red Riding Hood, The Butcher and His Wife, Jack and the Bean Stalk, etc.)

After Jack goes up the beanstalk, steals some items and kills the giant, the giant's wife (to avenge the death of her husband) comes down the beanstalk and terrorizes the kingdom. Before they come together, the people point their fingers at each other blaming one another for their woes.

One of the best scenes/songs (in my opinion) is *"It's Your Fault"*

Every time I hear this song, I cannot help but think of the exchanges so many of us have — *"It's your fault!"*, *"No it isn't, it's yours!"*

We are so quick to point the finger of blame looking for the fault line. But there is so much fault and too many fault lines to follow.

What we forget is that the more fault lines, the greater likelihood of earthquake.

I read a post today about a Black Lives Matter group that did not want white people to participate. It got me to thinking.

There are very few advantages to getting older. For the most part, getting older comes with new challenges that include brittle bones, loss of balance, the inability to do so many things that we could do when we were young. But there are also advantages. Chief among those advantages is perspective: the ability to look back at a long life and see what has changed, and what has not; to have seen different things tried, some of which failed and some of which succeeded. Through the lens of older eyes, we see things today that we may not have seen ten, twenty or thirty years ago.

It is true that any private group has the right to refuse to admit people into its ranks and/or events for any reason whatsoever. Insofar as it is not state-sanctioned, self-segregation along any identity-lines is perfectly legal.

But, just because something is legal, does not make it morally right. For example, even if legal, it is not morally acceptable for a golf course or country club to exclude people based on race, gender or religion, etc.

Does anyone remember being bussed to a different area so that we could end state-sanctioned segregation in schools? I do. And I wonder:

Why did so many people struggle for so long and so hard to end state-sanctioned segregation if only to engage in self-segregation? Do they not remember the struggle?

I guess that is the advantage of older eyes: the ability to see things through a long lens.

Does anyone else remember?

I remember the first time I heard the word *"bitch"* used on television. It was the mid to late 1980s. Up until that time, nobody would have dared to say that word on the air for fear that they would be fined by the FCC. The first time I heard the word on television, was on an episode of *"Designing Women"* and it was in the context of a joke about the differences between the North and the South. It went something like this:

At a party, the Southern girl walked up to the Northern girl and asked, *"Where ya'll from?"*

The Northern girl replied, *"We are from the place where we do not end our sentences in prepositions."*

The Southern girl thought for a moment, and then responded, *"Ok. So, where ya'll from, bitch?"*

As one can imagine, it was quite shocking in the 1980s that such profanity was used on public airwaves. Of course, many were quick to point out that this was how people truly spoke in the real world.

Fast forward to today. A couple of weeks ago, I was watching some sitcom on one of the three big networks, i.e., public airwaves. The main character used the word *"fuck"* at least four times. Something that would have been unheard of twenty years ago. Now, the word was bleeped out and the actor's mouth was blurred, but the intent and meaning was clear to the viewer. And many are quick to point out, this is how people truly speak in the real world.

But I cannot help but wonder: Is our art a reflection of the coarsening of American culture? Or, is the coarsening of American culture a reflection of our art?

Which came first, the chicken or the egg?

JUNE 10, 2017

The movie *"All About Eve"* is about an aging actress dealing with her own insecurities and the machinations of a younger actress trying to steal her limelight. When the aging actress complains about the younger actress to her boyfriend, he says to her in response:

"Have you no human consideration?"

She retorts, *"Show me a human and I might have."*

Great dialogue and funny exchange.

But . . . in her retort, what the character misses is that human consideration, human kindness, human compassion are not things one shows to another person because that person is a human being. Rather, these are qualities one displays toward another because the one displaying the quality is one. It is showing these qualities that makes us human.

When we denigrate and ridicule another and treat them as if they are not human, we are not dehumanizing them. We dehumanize ourselves.

June 16, 2017

I had another lucid dream the other night.

Since I dislocated my shoulder, I cannot sleep on my left side — only on my back or the right, at least until it heals. I was asleep on my right side when something crawled into bed and snuggled up against my chest wanting me to hold it and sleep with it. It scared me, but I could not push it away or wake up. Finally, after a few deep breaths (in my sleep-mind) I was able to wake. Of course, there was nothing snuggled up against me.

It took another hour before I could fall back to sleep.

It must be time to light the candles.

JUNE 22, 2017

I was reading about the competing plans about repeal-and-replace of Obamacare and I could not help but think:

Way back, when the world was young and God was yet a boy, I first obtained health insurance through my employer. I had to pay the bill and then submit a claim to the insurance company. Health care providers did not care what coverage I had, because I paid them. It was up to me to seek reimbursement from my insurance company if I had such coverage.

In later years, that changed. Health care providers entered into agreements with various insurers and began submitting the claims directly. I no longer saw the bill except in some lengthy *"explanation of benefits"* document. In exchange for the HCP submitting the claim, they were guaranteed payment at the agreed upon rate. But, the consumer of the service was divorced from the financial aspects of that service. The result: $12 aspirin during a hospital stay. The consumer had no idea that the HCP was charging $12 for that medication, because he or she never saw or paid attention to the bill as it was covered by the insurance company.

One of the great deceptions over the last ten or fifteen years has been the so-called debate over healthcare. It is a deception because nobody is debating health *care*. The politicians (and the country) is debating health *insurance coverage*. Nobody is denied healthcare insofar as he or she is willing to pay for it. In fact, it is illegal to deny coverage at all if one goes to a county hospital's emergency room. So, the argument is: who is responsible for paying for the care?

- Should insurance companies be on the hook for covering individuals who have paid little or no premiums?

- Should the taxpayer be on the hook for subsidizing individuals of low to moderate incomes?

- Should individuals be forced by government mandate to carry coverage that they neither want nor need (for example, maternity care for a seventy year old, or birth control pills for a celibate male)?

In our knee jerk reactions for (or against) reform, we have lost sight of what the debate is about. There is no doubt in my mind that we need a system in place that guarantees that nobody is denied coverage for inability to pay. But the question — the argument — is: what system ensures that people are not denied service, while still ensuring that health care providers are paid a fair value for the services rendered? And who is responsible to pay for those services?

Let's stop kidding ourselves. This is not a debate about healthcare. This is a debate about who pays for the healthcare. What insures as opposed to ensures?

June 25, 2017

Sir John Dalberg-Acton was an English historian, politician, and writer. He is best known for the quote, *"Power tends to corrupt, and absolute power corrupts absolutely. Great men are almost always bad men . . ."* He said this because *"great men"* necessarily wield power, and that power ultimately corrupts and destroys them. Lord Acton made an excellent point about the corruption of power. Those in power, no matter how well meaning they initially may be, invariably begin to wield their power in a way that benefits themselves, their family and their friends. They forget about the simple man that gave them the power in the first place.

But, in my opinion, Lord Acton had it only partly right. Power does corrupt. However, I think that Aung San Suu Kyi was closer to the truth. She is a Burmese politician and author who was the first woman to serve as Minister of Foreign Affairs and Minister of the President's Office in the country of Myanmar. She said: *"It is not power that corrupts but fear. Fear of losing power corrupts those who wield it and fear of the scourge of power corrupts those who are subject to it."*

But given all of the above, I still believe that David Brin (an American scientist and science fiction writer) made the most poignant observation when he wrote in his book *The Postman* that: "*It is said that power corrupts, but actually it's more true that power attracts the corruptible. The sane are usually attracted by other things than power.*"

Too often, Americans wear their ideological blinders and proclaim that this politician or that one is "*corrupt.*" Usually, the allegation is made more out of political opposition than true corruption. At the same time that we decry the "*corrupt*" politicians on the other side of the aisle, we excuse the same "*corrupt*" actions on the part of the politicians that we glorify and, often beatify. With our blinders securely in place, we refuse to see their "*corrupt*" actions for what they are — after all, we support them.

As we watch the political parties in Washington jockey for position and power, they often are corrupted by the power they seek. And those that have power, are often corrupted by the fear of losing it.

American citizens are, in fact, the guardians of our Republic. It is our sacred obligation as guardians to put away our ideological blinders and to see the men and women to whom we give authority as the people that they are. It is important that we bear in mind that those who seek power may, in fact, seek that power because, as Brin said, "*Power attracts the corruptible.*" And it's important that we see these men and women who, no matter how well meaning they may be, are likely to fall to the temptation that power promotes either out of desire or out of fear.

We must put away the ideological blinders and see that the politicians we hold out as heroes are subject to the same potential for corruption as those we hold out as foes.

My mother probably said it best when she said: "*When a man puts himself in temptation's way, sooner or later he will be tempted.*"

JUNE 27, 2017

All insurance is legalized gambling.

Life insurance is a gamble that you will pay the insurer more before you die, then they pay out when you do.

Car insurance is a gamble that that you will pay the insurer more in premiums, then you ever collect on a claim.

Social Security insurance is a gamble that you will die, before you collect.

JUNE 28, 2017

"In an insane world, the sane man must appear insane." ~C. William King.

June 29, 2017

Upon their deaths, in their last will and testament, our forefathers bequeathed to us, the American people, a system of governance that has withstood over 200 years of challenges. That system provided avenues for change as necessary.

I have often opined on the ruling oligarchy in our nation. It has been my belief that the political parties don't rule this nation, but neither does the executive, legislative or judicial branches of government. In fact, it is my belief that the ruling oligarchy is the unaccountable entrenched bureaucracy that has developed, over time, since the inception of this nation. With each successive election, that bureaucracy has grown. The entrenched interests of these unelected, unaccountable individuals prevail, and the average citizen is left with no choice but to succumb to the decisions that are made by the faceless, nameless bureaucrat. Put another way, *"You can't fight City Hall."* The only way to remove the oligarchy is to dismantle the bureaucracy that gave way to its rise.

It is a fundamental precept of any civilized nation that the citizenry of that nation agrees to live under the rule of law. If the law is unjust, then there are avenues for changing that law. Of course, one must traverse the murky waters of bureaucracy to do so.

That said, when we, as a people, begin to accept the notion that individuals may resort to methods of self-help in fighting the bureaucracy, we have ceded to the forces of darkness our right to call ourselves a civilized society. Where individuals or groups of individuals feel that it is "*ok*" to destroy property or harm persons with whom they disagree on policy, we are no longer a civilized society.

Mob rule is just as bad as rule by an oligarchy.

Anyone who would support the destruction of a monument as described in the recent story regarding the Ten Commandments in Arkansas has lost sight of the fundamental precepts of what it means to be a civilized society.

Anyone who would support the so-called protests that are, in actuality, riots and/or destruction of personal property (as recently displayed on way too many campuses across this great nation of ours) has lost sight of the fundamental precepts of democracy.

We can disagree on policy positions without destroying society in the process. We can work together to come to compromise — even when the positions appear diametrically opposed to each other. All that is needed is the will to do so.

When did we lose the will?

JUNE 30, 2017

In each life, there are hours of agony, but it is the moments of pure bliss that make enduring worth the while. Treasure the moments.

July 4, 2017

In recent days, it has become quite fashionable among certain quarters of society, among certain celebrities, academic intelligentsia, media figures, and politicians to bash the United States of America and loudly proclaim her flaws. But, today, is not the day for that. Today is the day to remember and to celebrate the reason for her existence and the principles that form her foundation.

Two hundred and forty-one years ago, our forefathers declared the independence of this great nation. They set forth on paper the basic precepts that are meant to be the foundation of our society. These great men knew that decency and integrity required that, before taking the extraordinary step of declaring independence, they set forth their grievances against the tyranny from which they sought freedom stating, in the introductory paragraph to that declaration, that: *"A decent respect to the opinions of mankind requires that they should declare the causes which impel them to the separation."*

In their indictment of British Crown, they accused King George of the following abuses, among others:

261

"He has refused his assent to laws, the most wholesome and necessary for the public good.

"He has forbidden his governors to pass laws of immediate and pressing importance . . . till his assent should be obtained; and . . .

"He has called together legislative bodies at places unusual, uncomfortable, and distant . . . for the sole purpose of fatiguing them into compliance . . .

"He has obstructed the administration of justice, by refusing his assent to laws for establishing judiciary powers . . .

"He has erected a multitude of new offices, and sent . . . swarms of officers to harass our people . . .

"He has kept among us, in times of peace, standing armies without the consent of our legislature . . .

"He has combined with others to subject us to a jurisdiction foreign to our constitution, and unacknowledged by our laws . . ." [such as]

". . . quartering large bodies of armed troops among us . . ." and ". . protecting them, by mock trial . . .

". . . For cutting off our trade . . .

". . . For imposing taxes on us without our consent. . .

". . . For depriving us in many cases, of the benefits of trial by jury:

". . . For taking away our charters, abolishing our most valuable laws, and altering fundamentally the forms of our governments . . ."

Upon issuing this indictment of the Crown, they declared that a people has the right to self-determination.

They declared that, *"certain unalienable rights"* including the rights to life, liberty and the pursuit of happiness are rights not conferred by government, but rather bestowed upon man by his Creator.

They declared that in order to secure those rights, governments are *"instituted among men, deriving their just powers from the consent of the governed."*

On this 241st anniversary of the adoption of this resolution, today would be a good day to read this document and remind ourselves what we are all about.

The full text can be found at http://www.ushistory.org/declaration/document/

July 4, 2017

I wept for the man without his voice,
Until I learned that was his choice.

I wept for the man who had no touch,
Until I learned that was his crutch.

I wept for the man who had no heart,
Until I learned that was his tart.

I wept for the man who had no mind,
Until I learned he was disinclined.

I wept for the man who had no soul,
Until I learned that was his goal.

I wept for the man who could not see,
Until I learned that man was me.

I wept for the man who could not cry,
Until I learned that man was I.

"God is dead. God remains dead. And we have killed him . . . What was holiest and mightiest of all that the world has yet owned has bled to death under our knives: who will wipe this blood off us? . . . Must we ourselves not become gods simply to appear worthy of it?" ~ Nietzsche, *The Gay Science*, Section 125.

In his work, *"The Gay Science,"* Nietzsche wrote that God is dead. Man, in his hubris, killed off the concept of God and set himself up in His stead.

But, I do not believe that God is dead. I think He has just had enough and turned away. Maybe it is His own form of tough love against mankind.

"In individuals, insanity is rare; but in groups, parties, nations and epochs, it is the rule." ~Friedrich Nietzsche

JULY 15, 2017

I grow so weary of hearing the 99% complain about their trials and tribulations. The 1% have their problems too. Like, just this morning, while in the shower, I had to stand on my toes to shave because the maid moved my shaving mirror an inch too high.

#oldgaydisabledhalfbreedprivilege

Is our society really that mean-spirited?

Is our society really that cruel?

Is our society really that obnoxious?

Is our society doomed?

A couple of days ago, the news broke that Sen. John McCain was diagnosed with glioblastoma ". . . *A fast-growing, aggressive type of central nervous system tumor that forms on the supportive tissue of the brain.*" (See, http://www.cancercenter.com/brain-cancer/types/tab/glioblastoma-multiforme/)

According to www.abta.org "[w]*ith standard treatment, median survival . . . [f]or adults with more aggressive glioblastoma . . . is about 14.6 months and two-year survival is 30%.*" (See, http://www.abta.org/brain-tumor-information/types-of-tumors/glioblastoma.html)

Sen. McCain will be undergoing treatment. Regardless of political perspective, my prayers go out to him and to his family. I wish him a full and speedy recovery and hope that his family finds comfort during this trying time.

It saddens me that, yesterday morning, I woke to posts on social media decrying Sen. McCain. One such post actually asked whether it was wrong to *"pray"* that all the Republican members of Congress contract this disease, while another post stated that, ". . . *[i]f he* [McCain] *votes to repeal Obamacare, then just let the selfish POS die."*

Regardless of one's political affiliation, nobody should ever be treated so callously. Even if, in our callousness, we cannot show a modicum of decency and respect to the person that is ill, we should at least afford comfort to the family of the one that is suffering. Whatever one's disagreement with the person that is ill, his family had nothing to do with it. After all, as John Donne wrote (see my May post) *"No man is an island."*

And I am left to wonder:

Is our society really that mean-spirited? I could say that I am appalled, because I am.

Is our society really that cruel? I could say that I am dismayed, because I am.

Is our society really that obnoxious? I could say that I am surprised . . . but I am not.

If this is what we have become, then our society really is doomed.

July 26, 2017

I saw a post from a man who complained about caring for is ill mother. And, I wonder, who shall care for the custodians?

For a little boy, his custodian was his mother. She fed, clothed and sheltered him from the time he was born until the time that he was able to care for himself. She asked very little in return.

"Why do you do this?" he asked, *"You have your own life to live and this is too heavy a burden."*

"It is my job," she said, *"to do these things."*

As the boy grew, he watched as she and his father cared for each other — *"in sickness and in health"* as they say. And in the days following his father's diagnosis with a particularly horrendous disease, he watched as his mother cared for this man; a man who had once been a tower of strength, until the day the man passed from this world.

"Why do you do this?" he asked, *"You have your own life to live and this is too heavy a burden."*

"It is my job," she said, *"to do these things."*

As a young adult, he watched as his mother cared for his aging grandparents; her parents, now too old and sick to care for themselves. She sacrificed her time, energy and effort to ensure that they were cared for.

"Why do you do this?" he asked, *"You have your own life to live and this is too heavy a burden."*

"It is my job," she said, *"to do these things."*

True love is sacrifice. It is putting the needs of another above one's own wants and desires. Who will care for us when we are old, sick or just need help? Why do we do this? We have our own lives to live and this is too heavy a burden.

"It is my job," she said, *"to do these things."*

Who shall care for the custodians?

July 28, 2017

We have all heard the story of Adam and Eve. They lived in innocence in the Garden of Eden until that day that Eve, tempted by the serpent, ate fruit from the forbidden Tree of Knowledge. In so doing, she released a scourge of evil on this world that led to the couple being cast out from paradise.

But, I believe that it was actually Adam who ate fruit from the Tree of Knowledge. In so doing, he learned how to blame it on Eve.

Now you know the real story.

When the guy on TV said he might be able to give two inches, I did not think I would be satisfied with that. But if all he can give is two inches, I will take it.

I am talking about rain, of course. Get your minds out of the gutter!

Is our society too wealthy?

Here are seven signs that society is too rich:

1. We pay to go to a gym to work hard, rather than build our muscles by hard work.

2. We hire others to do what we can do for ourselves.

3. We complain about small things, because we have nothing larger to complain about.

4. We are more concerned about looking good than we are about being good.

5. We rent storage units because our houses are not large enough to hold our things.

6. We complain that there is not enough time to meet all of our social engagements.

7. We take our pets to a psychotherapist.

I admit to being guilty of more than one of the above. Can you think of others?

AUGUST 6, 2017

My rowdy friends are going out on the boat, but since I can't climb in or out right now, I guess I will have to be satisfied with an in-home massage.

#oldgaydisabledhalfbreedprivilege

I read a commentary about the possible senatorial run of *"Kid Rock"* which opined that (with the election of Donald Trump) American culture has become so coarse such that we are prepared to elect *"reality stars"* to public office.

With all due respect to the author, this should come as no surprise. American culture has been on the decline for decades and its coarsening has only been hastened in recent years. From the *"free love"* movement of the 1960s to the *"me generation"* of the 1970s. From the cocaine and crack abuse of the 1980s to the *"I did not have sex with that woman . . ."* of the 1990s. And on, and on, and on.

Our culture has been turned on its head. Consider that, not very long ago, smoking tobacco was acceptable and smoking marijuana was criminal. Today, recreational marijuana is legal in some states and so-called medical marijuana is rampant, while at the same time, governmental agencies pass more and more restrictive regulations on the use of tobacco.

Where once, angels were considered good (remember *"Highway to Heaven"* with Michael Landon?) and vampires were evil (recall, Stephen King's *"Salem's Lot"*?), today, vampires are depicted as mere tortured souls fighting their sanguine addiction (*"Twilight"*, *"True Blood"*, etc.) and angels are depicted as evil (the movies *"Prophecy"* and *"Legion"*).

With the dissemination of more and more so-called reality shows that depict people in the least flattering of light, is it any surprise that our culture has become increasingly coarse? Is it any surprise that our culture has become increasingly corrupt?

I cannot help but wonder: Is our art a reflection of the coarsening of American culture? Or, is the coarsening of American culture a reflection of our art?

The author of the above-referenced commentary seems surprised that *"Kid Rock"* could be considered a viable contender for US Senate, but I am not. We get the leaders that we deserve. We get the leaders that reflect our values. If our art and our values are increasingly coarse, it is any wonder that our culture is? If our people are increasingly coarse, is it any wonder that our leaders are? After all, our leadership is selected from those among us.

For a free society to exist, its citizens must be free to create, free to produce, free to distribute, free to earn, free to choose. They must be free to think. They must be free to do these things unfettered by an overreaching central authority.

The American experiment is premised upon the ideal of individual freedom. In fact, the first ten amendments to the Constitution, (the so-called Bill of Rights) were adopted to ensure this. At her core, America is an ideal that individuals, each and every one, have the right to freedom of political thought, ideology and expression; that each and every citizen has the freedom to determine his or her own fate, in large part, by the freedom to choose his or her own path; that government is instituted solely to protect this freedom. Its purpose is not to tell its citizenry what it must do, but rather to ensure that its citizenry has the right to choose for themselves.

It seems that recently, I have seen an increasing number of social media posts indicting capitalism. In fact, our nation has been witness to protests and even riots in our streets that call for the end to capitalism in America in favor of a socialist economic system. I believe this is misguided.

To understand, we must first define these terms.

According to Merriam-Webster:

Capitalism is:

1 *"an economic system characterized by private or corporate ownership of capital goods, by investments that are determined by private decision, and by prices, production, and the distribution of goods that are determined mainly by competition in a free market"*

Socialism is:

1 *"any of various economic and political theories advocating collective or governmental ownership and administration of the means of production and distribution of goods*

2 a: a system of society or group living in which there is no private property

b: a system or condition of society in which the means of production are owned and controlled by the state

3 a stage of society in Marxist theory transitional between capitalism and communism and distinguished by unequal distribution of goods and pay according to work done"

Communism is:

"a : a theory advocating elimination of private property

2 b : a system in which goods are owned in common and are available to all as needed"

Put simply, capitalism is premised upon private ownership and private decisions. Under this economic system, each individual can own, produce and distribute products as he chooses (consistent with applicable laws that protect the populace as a whole). While socialism and communism are each premised upon collective, public ownership and decisions. In other words, there is no private ownership and a central authority makes decisions as it relates to the prices, production and distribution of goods. Communism goes a step further than socialism in that it dictates that everything that is created, manufactured and produced is done so according to the ability of the creator, manufacturer and producer, and that the end product is publicly owned and distributed according to the needs of the individual. That distribution is dictated by the State.

When comparing these three economic systems, it becomes clear that only capitalism marries with the ideal of American freedom. It is the only one of these three that advocates for private ownership and private decision-making. (That is not to say that government regulations should not be instituted, but rather, that any such regulations that are adopted, should be adopted to ensure the continuation of individual rights and that, where such rights are limited, they are limited only to protect individuals from the abuses of others.) Capitalism is the only system that does not take away choice. It is the system that empowers individuals to choose. And freedom is premised upon the right to choose.

Without economic choice, there is no economic freedom. Without economic freedom there is no political choice. Without political choice, there is no political freedom. Without choice, there is no freedom, and one cannot survive, without the other.

Contrast that to the socialist and communist models. In these models, the economic system does not protect individual freedom. To the contrary, each of these models are premised upon the idea that the state dictates the decisions made. They are designed to take away private ownership and private decision-making. Each of these models are premised on the idea that the State knows better than the individual; that the State chooses for the individual. By their very nature, they run contrary to our great nation's founding ideology: the freedom of the individual to choose. The only true freedom is the right to choose. All other freedoms stem from that.

As I read the aforementioned posts or watch the aforementioned protests and riots on television each night, I am left to wonder why the advocates for these other economic models do not understand this. Why do they have such a gross misunderstanding of these three economic models and the consequences that are inherent in each?

Is this the result of a failed educational system; a system that has refused to teach this generation the very definition of these systems? Is this the result of individual failure to learn that one is premised on choice and freedom, while the other two are premised on authoritarian control?

Is it that, having been free to make their own choices their entire lives, the advocates do not understand the consequences of taking away choice?

Is it that these advocates simply follow the latest trend?

Or, perhaps, they fully understand, but are intent on remaking the nation into an authoritarian regime?

I do not know the reason, but whatever it may be, the future of free society is at stake. After all, for a free society to exist, its citizens must be free to create, free to produce, free to distribute, free to earn, free to choose. They must be free to think. They must be free to do these things unfettered by an overreaching central authority.

The citizenry must be free.

August 11, 2017

When I was in school, all children had a dress code that included no bare shoulders. Girls could wear skirts, but they could not be short skirts. Neither gender was allowed to wear shorts except in gym class. Boys could not wear earrings and the jewelry that girls wore had to be tasteful and modest so as not to distract anyone. Boys could not have long hair; it could not touch their collar and they had to be clean shaven. And yes, all shirts had to be tucked in and had to have collars; no t-shirts (except in gym class). Nobody was allowed to wear open-toed shoes. Hats and sunglasses were not permitted indoors. Children dressed for school as if they were headed to their place of employment, because going to school was considered the child's job. We were not allowed to dress as if we were going to the park, the lake or a pool party. Proper dress was a sign of respect for those around you.

Of course, I am old. But it seems to me that the issue of inappropriate dress in school could be solved if:

1) parents taught their children that one does not dress as if they are going to a pool party when they go to school; and,

2) if the school enforced reasonable dress standards on both genders.

Or maybe the best answer is requiring school uniforms. Then nobody could bitch, moan or complain about what they can or cannot wear and maybe, just maybe, Little Johnny would know how to read when he graduated.

August 12, 2017

So, I did not sleep well last night; plagued, as I was, by lucid dreams. Actually, they were lucid nightmares.

We went to bed around 11:30 which is a little late for us. At 2:30 in the morning, I was aware that I was dreaming. In the dream, I was lying in bed and the shadow of a little girl who was walking around the bed with a lilting laughter while staring at me and my partner. In my mind's eye, I followed her progress as she kept playing this game of ring-around-the-rosy. Then another figure emerged; this one larger, darker and menacing. It followed her around the bed listening to her laughter. That is, until he noticed that I was watching. Then he drew closer to me and began rubbing my shoulder, until finally, he crawled into the bed and on top of me. He was not trying to smother me, it was like he was trying to merge himself into me. Goosebumps ran up and down my arms and even my back, and I forced myself awake. But I was so creeped out, I could not go back to sleep.

So, I stepped outside and had a smoke before returning indoors, then turned on the television and lied down my on the sofa. I hoped that the familiar sounds of back-to-back *Cheers* re-runs would lull me into sleep. And that worked, until I again realized that I was in the throes of yet another lucid dream; this time, staring at an old book that the figure was holding in front of me as I lie on the sofa. He wanted me to read from it, but I did not want to.

Again, I forced myself awake. It was now 4:30 in the morning. I stepped out for another smoke and returned inside. This time, I told the shadow in my mind to leave me alone. *"I am tired,"* I said. If you have something to say, come tell me in the morning.

I fell into a fitful sleep on the sofa waking every half-hour or so. No more shadows and no more lucid dreams. Until finally, around 6:00 a.m., I arose and made my morning coffee.

Next Monday, August 21, large swaths of our nation will bear witness to the Great American Total Solar Eclipse. The skies will darken and the light will go out. This will be the first total solar eclipse visible from the lower 48 since 1979 and the first one that will be visible from coast to coast since 1918 almost one hundred years ago. Many people and communities that are in the path of the totality of this eclipse will be hosting *"eclipse parties."* Others, are traveling to these more desirable locations to witness first-hand the event.

Today, we know the cause, but for most of human history, mankind was devoid of this understanding. In centuries past, people watched these solar eclipses with fear and trepidation. Some ancient peoples were convinced that a solar eclipse was an omen of celestial warfare where ancient gods fought amongst themselves. Some believed that the eclipse was a portent of evil to come; an apocalypse that would rain down upon them. To thwart this evil, they held great *"hullabaloos"* (the making of noise, dancing and acting insane) all in the hope of scaring away the demons.

As I reflect on this and consider the last few years, I cannot help but wonder on the lessons we failed to learn from the ancients. As this eclipse approaches, we witness a people who seemingly has lost its sense of propriety, its sense of decency, its sense of good will toward our fellow man. We choose to hate those that are different in race, creed, color, gender or orientation. We choose to hate those who have different thoughts and ideas. We degrade and denigrate those with whom we disagree on each and every topic, seemingly unable even to agree to disagree.

In the name of God, or for the cause of religion or for the ideas expressed in philosophy and politics, we torture, maim and kill. We do this even in the name of tolerance, seemingly unable to understand that word's very definition.

Our guardians kill those they are meant to guard. Our people kill the guardians. Our community fights within itself as if trying to commit suicide. All the while our leaders fail to lead, instead choosing to fan the fires of this hatred for their own sport.

And I fear. I fear that perhaps the light has gone out before the darkening of the sun.

Our people make noise, dance and generally act insane. I cannot help but wonder, what is this hullabaloo all about? Clearly, it is not scaring away the demons.

August 13, 2017

He was born fifty years ago, the progeny of a white man and a Mexican-American woman. Throughout the entirety of his life he was referred to as the *"half-breed."*

As he watched the news reports hearing alternately how Mexicans were taking American jobs or how white people were the cause of the ills of society, he could not help but wonder: Am I the oppressed or am I the oppressor? Is it possible to oppress myself?

Because I voted third party last November, some have told me that I threw away and wasted my vote. So, I ask them, "*Who did you vote for?*"

And when they tell me, regardless of the answer, I just laugh and laugh.

Sometimes, it seems that we become so concerned with saving a burning tree, that we do not see the forest fire raging around us.

Three men are on the sea in a boat that has sprung a leak.

One guys says, *"We need to bail out the water from the boat or else we will sink."*

The second guy says, *"We need to plug the leak first, then bail out the water."*

The third guy says, *"I wanted to go swimming anyway."*

SEPTEMBER 2, 2017

We returned from our trip to Romania getting home last night after eighteen hours of travel. What a fascinating trip! We had so much fun, eating and drinking with the locals. Talking with others we met who were visiting from as far away as Kuwait and Lebanon and Finland and Spain.

We visited so many of the historic sites.

In Constanta, we saw some ruins from ancient Rome that were erected after the region's final conquest by the emperor Trajan. I asked the tour guide about that period of time in their history. *"We think . . ."* she said, but *"we do not know for certain . . ."* Succeeding generations and conquerors destroyed much of the ancient documents, structures and monuments, so little is really known.

After Rome departed from the region, Romania was conquered and controlled by various peoples including the Goths, the Huns, the Gepis, the Avara, the Cumans and the Uzes. I asked our guide about those times. *"We think . . ."* she said, but *"we do not know for certain . . ."* Succeeding generations and conquerors destroyed much of the ancient documents, structures and monuments, so little is really known.

We visited an old church and old Mosque. We visited Bran castle (built in 1212) and romanticized as *"Dracula's castle"* although Vlad the Impaler (considered the source of the Dracula legends) really had little to no connection to that castle. I asked about those times. *"We think . . ."* she said, but *"we do not know for certain . . ."* Succeeding generations and conquerors destroyed much of the ancient documents, structures and monuments, so little is really known.

We visited Peles Castle - the retreat of the Romanian royalty in the 1800s and were told fascinating stories about the Germanic family that formed the monarchy. I asked about those times. *"We think . . ."* she said, but *"we do not know for certain . . ."* Succeeding generations and conquerors destroyed much of the ancient documents, structures and monuments, so little is really known.

Romania was a relatively new state sandwiched between the Austro-Hungarian and Russian empires at the start of World War I. The nation remained neutral for the first two years; that is until it joined the fray of that war in 1916. In 1920, most of its regions were finally united into one nation under the Treaty of Saint Germain and the Treaty of Paris. I asked about those times. *"We think . . ."* she said, but *"we do not know for certain . . ."* Succeeding generations destroyed much of the documents, structures and monuments, so little is really known.

Initially, during World War II, Romania tried to remain neutral, but ultimately was pressured into joining in the war on the side of the Axes; that is until they switched sides toward the end of the War and joined the Allies. But it was too late for Romania, the communists aided by the Soviet armies, seized control of the government. Romania, became a communist dictatorship in 1947. The communists pursued brutal policies to enforce their ideals on the people and encouraged families to spy on each other. The educational system was geared to teach only those communist ideals. Many intellectuals, artists and others that had, before this time enjoyed a certain freedom and renaissance in their writings and art were forced to flee the country. I asked about those times. *"We think . . ."* she said, but *"we do not know for certain . . ."* Succeeding generations destroyed much of the documents, structures and monuments, so little is really known. The communists wanted to control the history of their nation.

In 1968, Nicolae Ceausescu became the communist leader in Romania. He continued the brutal policies. By all accounts from our tour guide (old enough to remember and recite the times) Ceausescu and his wife lived in luxury while the people suffered many deprivations common of communist era dictatorships, including long lines for commonplace items and electricity (controlled by the government) was shut off at 10 pm so that the state could save money. To finance some of his policies, Ceausescu *"sold"* emigration visas to Israel so that Jewish people could leave Romania and move to that state. Romania's Jewish population (once 800,000 at the start of WWII) has dwindled to about 3,000. I asked about those times. *"We think . . ."* she said, but *"we do not know for certain . . ."* The communists destroyed much of the documents, structures and monuments, so little is really known.

In the 1980s, Ceausescu determined to build a grand parliament building. He embarked on its construction by first seizing land and homes from people in a large swath of Bucharest's center. These people were given smaller *"communist"* apartments in other areas around the city. Their homes were destroyed to build the parliament building. This led, in part, to a huge stray dog population. The people could not take their pet dogs from their homes to their smaller apartments, so the dogs were left to wander the streets of Bucharest on their own. Eventually, the government, in an attempt to solve the problem, began castrating and spaying all of these stray dogs when not killing them outright. Although our guide book warned us about the packs of stray dogs, in truth, we only saw one with the telltale yellow tag in his ear that indicated he had been caught and castrated by the government.

To achieve his economic goals and to build his parliament, Ceausescu imposed policies that impoverished Romanians and exhausted the Romanian economy. He extended the authority of the state and, much like the North Korean regime today, imposed a cult of personality. There were abuses and torture against the people from his political opponents to ordinary citizens. Between 60,000 and 80,000 political prisoners were detained as psychiatric patients and treated in some of the most sadistic ways by the secret security service *"doctors"*. About two million people were direct victims of Communist repression in Romania.

In 1989, Romanians revolted against this oppressive regime. The fall of communism had already occurred across the rest of Eastern Europe and on Christmas Day, 1989, after a two hour *"trial"* Ceausescu and his wife were executed. Romania declared itself a democracy.

I asked about those times. *"We think . . ."* she said, but *"we do not know for certain . . ."* The communists destroyed so much of the documents, structures and monuments, that little is really known. What is known, is known from the collective memory of those who are still alive today and remember the repression they suffered under the communist regime.

Today, Romania is a member of NATO and part of the EU. They continue to struggle with the headaches of their (very recent) revolution against communism. Some who are too young to remember the brutal oppression and deprivations of those days, even consider that the communist model might be good for their nation. The guarantee of a job, food and security is alluring, after all. But the older generation, the ones who remember, remain reticent to discuss this history and are still somewhat fearful of openly talking to strangers. Our Parliamentary tour guide was a woman named Ana who was old enough to remember those days. We could hear the anger in her voice over the deprivation and oppression that she still recalls.

I asked her about those times. *"We think . . ."* she said, but *"we do not know for certain . . ."* So many documents, structures and monuments were destroyed that little is really known.

Romania has a long, rich and storied history. But so much of it remains unknown. *"We think,"* they say, *"but we are not certain . . ."*

It is good to be home. After any vacation, when the wheels of the plane touch down on one's home soil, one feels a certain relief — happy to be on familiar ground. But when I turn on the news and see the stories of the destruction of documents, structures and monuments fight here in the United States; when I read about the potential criminalization of words in some states, I cannot help but wonder . . . two or three hundred years from now, when a guide is leading some tourists through the streets of some American city, if a tourist asks about *"those times,"* will the guide be able to answer? Or will he or she say: *"We think . . . but we do not know for certain. So many documents, structures and monuments were destroyed that little is really known."*

SEPTEMBER 9, 2017

Shame is what a man feels when judged harshly by another. Guilt is what one feels when judged harshly by himself.

SEPTEMBER 9, 2017

Signs of the Apocalypse

War on a large scale. ~Matthew 24:7; Revelation 6:4.

Famine. ~Matthew 24:7; Revelation 6:5, 6.

Great earthquakes. ~Luke 21:11.

Pestilences, or epidemics of "terrible diseases." ~Luke 21:11.

Increase of crime. ~Matthew 24:12.

Ruining of the earth by mankind. ~Revelation 11:18.

Running out of vodka when the liquor store is closed. ~Annie 09:9

September 11, 2017

In the year 2000, our nation was divided over the election. At that time, I thought that I had never seen such anger and hatred as that which was on full display in those last months of that year. Some five hundred votes separated the winner in that race from the defeated candidate, and for months thereafter, the nation argued and squabbled about those results. Some opined, *"He is not my president!"* and actively worked to thwart him. I wondered whether it was time for the nation to split apart. I thought to myself . . . what will it take for us to come together as one people and to speak with one voice again? Do we need a national disaster to do so? And I wept.

A mere eight months into that administration, America was attacked. Some heinous monsters killed over 3,000 people in a despicable act of cowardice. The petty squabbles subsided when the new president took to the bullhorn atop the rubble of the World Trade Center. It seemed that, finally, we would come together. But, alas, that did not last long. Within a few short weeks, the petty squabbles began anew. Some opining, in the most paranoid conspiracy theories, that the administration had actually caused the disaster. Some said that it was our due for centuries of oppression. The ensuing months (and years) were fraught with these divisions and arguments. I wondered whether it was time for the nation to split apart. I thought to myself . . . what will it take for us to come together as one people and to speak with one voice again? Do we need another national disaster to do so? And I wept.

In August 2005, one of America's beloved cities was hit with a horrific hurricane — a storm that devastated that city. I wondered whether this was the disaster that will bring us together. And for a short time thereafter, it seemed we might do so. But within days, the petty squabbles resumed. In the ensuing years, the nation was divided. We argued and fought among ourselves. I wondered whether it was time for the nation to split apart. I thought to myself . . . what will it take for us to come together as one people and to speak with one voice again? Do we need more disasters to remind us who we are? And I wept.

It was with great hope in 2008 that the nation elected its new president — a historical event — and it seemed that perhaps, we had finally moved on from our petty differences. But the ensuing years proved that hope misplaced. We remained divided. We fought and argued among ourselves. If one side said the sky was blue, the other insisted it was green. The politicians and media chose to emphasize our differences rather than that which is common. I wondered whether it was time for the nation to split apart. I thought to myself . . . what will it take for us to come together as one people and to speak with one voice again? And I wept.

The 2016 election was a tumultuous time. The nation, still divided, chose a new leader. In the events leading up to that election, the vitriol, hatred and anger that spewed forth from each side was astounding. I had not seen anything like it in my lifetime. And days after the election results were announced, some took to the streets in riots. Others complained on social media aided by a news media (whether out of a misplaced belief in their own superiority or a desire to drum up ratings, who knows?) The fighting, the arguing, anger, the vitriol, the hatred was palpable. As some in the state of California chose to put on the ballot a referendum for secession, I wondered whether they were right and it was, perhaps, time for the nation to split apart. I thought to myself . . . what will it take for us to come together as one people and to speak with one voice again? Do we need disaster after disaster to do so? And I wept.

In August of 2017, a monster hurricane hit the nations fourth most populous city and the surrounding areas. People died. Hundreds of thousands were deluged under water. I wondered if this was the national disaster that would bring us together. It seemed, for a brief moment, that it may. But within days, some were blaming the new administration for the disaster (as if any administration seven months in could be responsible for a natural disaster). Others opined, that the state of Texas got what it deserved for voting for the villain. Still another opined, *"Good. The hillbillies in Texas are dying."* I wondered whether it was time for the nation to split apart. I thought to myself . . . what will it take for us to come together as one people and to speak with one voice again? Is this national disaster not enough to do so? And I wept.

Two weeks later, on September 10, the state of Florida was hit with hurricane Irma. I wondered, could this one-two punch finally be the catalyst for coming together? But within hours of that storm making landfall, I see anger, vitriol and hatred spewing forth from so many. "*Florida deserves it*," some say. "*Why would anyone choose to live in hurricane prone areas?*" some ask. Some blame the administration. Some blame the politicians. The left blames the right. The right blames the left. Not for the first time, I wondered whether it was time for the nation to split apart. I thought to myself . . . what will it take for us to come together as one people and to speak with one voice again? Are these national disasters not enough? And I wept.

This morning marks the 16th anniversary of those horrendous events in 2001. Despite all of the reasons for us to come together, we seem unable to do so. We continue with our bickering, our anger and our hatred of "*the other*" — whomever that "*other*" may be.

And I wonder . . . if 9/11/2001 was not enough to bring us together; if Katrina, Harvey, Irma and so many other disasters along the way are not enough to bring us together; if these are not enough to cause us to put aside our petty differences to finally come together and speak with one voice — what will it take?

And I weep.

SEPTEMBER 16 2017

A long time ago, in a land far away . . .

There was a small town in the middle of the country. The town was made up of many different people and disparate groups. But once a week, the people of the town got together at the Town Common to discuss issues, socialize and otherwise enjoy the company of the other townsfolk.

Some of the townsfolk, however, did not like going to the Town Common. Situated, as it was, in the center of town, these folks found that the Common was simply too far from their homes or their own neighborhoods. Instead, they started meeting within their neighborhoods to discuss issues, socialize and otherwise enjoy the company of their neighbors. They called their neighborhood centers the Town Different.

The town center emptied and in time, the Town Common fell to disrepair from lack of use. The town was no longer one and fell apart.

When people go to the Different instead of the Common, the center cannot hold. It falls to disrepair from lack of use and the community is no longer one. The community falls apart.

SEPTEMBER 16, 2017

I saw a news report about the London subway so-called "bucket bomber." The news anchor asked the question: How can we stop these type of attacks? Of course, there were a number of responses from the panel. Basically, however, each agreed, we cannot stop them. If an individual is intent on murder and mayhem, he will find a way.

It got me to thinking how do we stop people from hurting each other?

I believe that the responsibility lies in our education. Currently, that education teaches and emphasizes the "*different*" in each other and forgets about what is common.

As a child, little Ahmad was educated in a Madrassa — not one of those radical Madrassa's that taught jihad. No, he was NOT taught that terrorism was acceptable. But, he was taught that those who did not believe as he did were "*different*" and that the "*different*" were evil. America was the Big Satan, Israel was the Little Satan and Jews . . . were evil. His educators extolled the virtues of peace and non-violence, but still, they taught him that others were evil. As an adult, Ahmad came to believe that it was his

308

responsibility to destroy evil. He became radicalized and turned to violence. You see, evil must be destroyed by any means necessary. And so he killed.

As a child, little Mary was educated by people who believed that homosexuality is a sin. She was NOT taught to hate homosexuals, she was told to *"hate the sin, but not the sinner."* She was taught that they were *"different."* She was taught that sin was evil. She came to believe that the *"different"* was evil. Her educators extolled the virtues of peace and non-violence, but still, they taught her that others were evil. As an adult, Mary came to believe that it was her responsibility to destroy evil. She became radicalized and turned to violence. You see, evil must be destroyed by any means necessary. And she killed.

As a child, little Marcus was educated in a system that taught him that America was made up of *"different"* groups. The Founding Fathers were evil white men who enslaved black people. The police intentionally killed black people and should be feared. The white man was the cause of all the social ills in America. He was NOT taught to do violence, but he was taught that white people were imbued with white privilege. He was taught that racism was evil and that all white people are inherently racists. He was taught that the *"different"* were evil. His educators extolled the virtues of peace and non-violence, but still, they taught him that others were evil. As an adult, Marcus came to believe that it was his responsibility to destroy evil. He became radicalized and turned to violence. You see, evil must be destroyed by any means necessary. And he killed.

When we teach children to seek the *"different"* they only find that which is *"different."*

When we teach children to only view the "*different*" they only see that which is "*different.*"

When we teach children that evil must be destroyed, they come to believe that it is their responsibility to destroy evil.

When we teach children that the "*different*" are evil, they come to believe they must destroy the "*different.*"

If we want to stop violence, hatred, anger and terrorism, we must first stop teaching our children that the "*different*" are evil.

If we want to stop violence, hatred, anger and terrorism, We must stop teaching our children that we are "*different.*"

We must stop emphasizing our different-ness and, instead, teach our common-ness.

If it walks like a duck and it quacks like a duck . . . it's probably a duck.

SEPTEMBER 18, 2017

Watching all of these television and movie personalities complain about a reality-star president might almost lead one to conclude they believe that celebrities should stay out of politics.

SEPTEMBER 20, 2017

If you narrowly cling to people who are like you;

If you narrowly cling to your own community;

If your entire world revolves only around a narrow community of people who think like you,

How will you learn about others?

If you want to have a narrow mind, have a narrow circle.

To broaden the mind, you must first broaden your circle.

The flag does NOT STAND for the government of the United States.

The flag does NOT STAND for the people of the United States.

The flag does NOT STAND for the men and women who have fought and died in our military.

The flag does NOT STAND for the administration in power.

The flag does NOT STAND for any man.

Rather,

The flag STANDS for the ideals upon which this nation was founded.

The flag STANDS for the idea that, "*All men are created equal.*"

The flag STANDS for the idea that, "*We are endowed . . . with certain inalienable rights . . .*"

The flag STANDS for the idea that we have the right to *"life, liberty and the pursuit of happiness."*

That some among us have failed and refused to live up to the ideals; that some among us have failed to implement those ideas at all times does not make the ideals and ideas any less valid.

Who among us would not STAND for the idea that, *"All men are created equal . . . endowed by their creator with certain inalienable rights, that among these are life, liberty and the pursuit of happiness"*?

The flag STANDS for these ideas. Why won't you?

Every zombie tale has a certain theme. If one pays attention, he will recognize the characteristics of the tale.

Zombies are created by infection with a virus. The virus focuses on propagating itself by infecting others. It feeds on the flesh of the uninfected.

The infected react to certain stimuli — sound, sight and smell. The zombie may stand dormant for a time until it is triggered by this stimuli; a loud noise, a movement or the scent of the uninfected. Once triggered, the zombie pursues its target with single-minded focus, that is, at least, until some other loud sound, movement or scent distracts it.

Another common characteristic of zombie tales is that the people are slow to recognize the threat of the virus. They cannot believe that such a virus exists — it's incredible, after all. The threat cannot be real! By the time they recognize the virus for what it is, it has already reached epidemic proportions.

The authorities are slow to respond to the epidemic. They cannot figure out the cause of the virus or how to cure it. When they finally recognize the threat and take effective measures to minimize it, the virus has reached pandemic proportions.

Eventually, the pandemic causes the downfall of society. It is the end to civilization as we know it. The survivors struggle to pick-up the pieces while still fighting the plague. They attempt to rebuild society, but the society they once knew and loved cannot be rebuilt. Who knows what new civilization will develop from the ashes of the old?

As we look around at our nation today, do we recognize the virus or will we stand by incredulous. The virus cannot be real, after all.

And yet . . . every zombie tale has a certain theme. If one pays attention, he will recognize the characteristics of the tale before it reaches pandemic proportions?

Can we?

September 26, 2017

Strange that those who claim they protest being disrespected and loudly proclaim how their offense, do not seem to mind disrespecting or offending others.

September 27, 2017

Perfection does not exist.

No thing is perfect. No idea, no thought, no philosophy nor ideology, no religion, no government, no nation, no person is perfect. Perfection does not exist.

If you honor and respect only that which is perfect, then you do not honor any idea, any thought, any philosophy or ideology, any religion, any government, any nation, any person. Perfection does not exist.

If you honor and respect only perfection, you honor and respect no thing.

If you honor and respect only perfection, you honor and respect nothing.

September 27, 2017

When Colin Kaepernick first took the knee, he said that he was protesting racial inequality in America and police brutality.

If you lean to the right, you were probably offended by his action. Not the protest, *per se,* but the method in which he chose to do so.

If you lean to the left, you probably supported his protest.

Donald Trump commented on the phenomena.

Now those who take a knee do so to protest Donald Trump and his comments.

Kinda lost the message there, didn't we?

You see, when you choose a divisive way to make a point, your point gets lost.

SEPTEMBER 28, 2017

Having seen so much of it, he had grown accustomed to bad behavior, such that he no longer recognized it.

SEPTEMBER 29, 2017

I read an online story about a librarian who refused some books from First Lady Melania Trump. Seriously? She refused a donation because she does not like the president?

As a small child, we grew up poor. We lived in a trailer park outside of Montopolis in Austin. For those who do not know, Montopolis was a poor *barrio* in the early 1970s. My mother, who had only a sixth-grade education, pushed and encouraged us to learn, to read. Of course, we could not afford to buy books. So, when the *"Reading is Fundamental"* group came to the school and gave out books, I got as many as I could. I wanted to read. I wanted to learn.

I can only imagine what may have happened to me if RIF had been prevented from donating those books because of someone's dislike for the donor.

It is a shame when a good gesture, such as giving books to children (or libraries that cater to them) becomes *"offensive"* to some.

Someday soon, humanity will cease to exist. The cause will not be what people think.

There will be no nuclear war. The lands will not slide under the rising seas of melting ice. There will be no environmental disaster. No asteroid will strike the planet. Machines will not rise up and take over.

No; humanity will die from a slow suicide, its signs so small, so insignificant that none recognize them. The seeds of discord, discontent and disharmony were planted so long ago. Those seeds have found fertile ground in the hearts of men too eager to spread anger, hatred and vitriol. They have grown into strangling vines that no amount of weeding can remove.

No, humanity will not end in some apocalyptic bang.

Humanity will end, because mankind has become so inhumane.

October 5, 2017

Any doctor worth his salt will tell you that treating the symptoms of a disease does not cure the disease. If you want to heal the body, you must cure the disease. And our society is suffering from a disease whose symptoms manifest in violence. But the disease is our propensity to demean, devalue and dehumanize each other.

Some would use violence to prevent so-called hate speech on campus — and half the country applauds.

Some would use violence to remove symbols they dislike — and half the country applauds.

Some would fail and refuse to respect the traditions and values upon which this nation was founded — and half the country applauds.

Some would even take to Twitter and say they have no sympathy for the victims of violence because those victims *"probably"* share a political philosophy with which they disagree — and half the country applauds.

Some would take to the airwaves or social media and call those with whom they disagree, *"libtard, repug, idiot, bitch, motherfucker"* and on and on and on — and half the country applauds.

We do this and we spread the infection.

Using guns in violence is a symptom. Treating that symptom with more gun control or stringent background checks only treats the symptom. It does not cure the disease.

Guns are not the problem. Lack of gun control is not the problem. The failure of background checks is not the problem. That there a mentally deranged individuals out there is not the problem.

No.

The problem is that we continue to demean, devalue and dehumanize each other — **that** is the disease. And we continue to spread that disease.

When we demean . . . we cease to have meaning.

When we devalue . . . we cease to have value.

When we dehumanize . . . we cease to be human.

As long as we continue to demean, devalue and dehumanize; as long as we continue to spread the disease, its symptoms will find a way manifest.

Any doctor worth his salt will tell you that treating the symptoms of a disease does not cure the disease. If you want to heal the body, you must cure the disease.

OCTOBER 7, 2017

We just had a state pass a law that said it would not enforce federal law or otherwise cooperate with the federal authorities in that law's enforcement.

When was the last time something like that happened? Was it the 1860s? I wonder what happened back then.

Those who do not remember history are doomed to repeat it.

OCTOBER 8, 2017

It's boss's day. Be sure to send something to your wife.

Thinking . . .

Thinking . . .

Thinking . . .

No, don't say it.

While half of the nation has fallen on its knees to protest one thing, the other half has fallen on its knees to protest another. Regardless on which side one stands, the nation has fallen on its knees.

There are so many on social media who would benefit from a good dictionary:

cognitive dissonance.

Look it up.

October 21, 2017

The little dog was enraged. The neighborhood children were blowing the dog whistle again. For hours, they blew that whistle laughing at the little dog's fits. The dog ran around the room trying to find the source of that incessant sound. Barking and barking, he hoped to make it stop.

Meanwhile, in the upstairs bedroom, a faulty electrical wire sparked. The flames that started in the wall soon began to spread threatening to engulf the entire home. The family slept unaware that their lives were in peril. Despite the smoke that filled the room and despite the heat that he began to feel emanating from its walls, the little dog continued to chase after the sound of that whistle. He did not smell the smoke or feel the heat, consumed as he was by the sound of that whistle. The fire spread from the walls of that bedroom down to the walls of the kitchen and living room and soon beyond. It overtook the floor and the ceiling. And still the family slept.

The media is that dog, hearing nothing but the whistle. The house is the country and the flames are the threats we face. The family is the populace that continues to sleep.

Something must be wrong with my cable. I turned on the news this morning, and the only sound that emanated from the speakers was a bunch of dogs barking at a whistle that nobody else could hear.

Will we see the flames or chase the whistle?

NOVEMBER 4, 2017

At 2:00 a.m., tomorrow morning, we turn our clocks back one hour.

If only it were that easy to turn back time, but if it were . . . would you do it?

Let's see if my math checks out . . .

On March 12 the government took an hour from me. That is 60 minutes. They are returning it to me tomorrow morning. That is 238 days. At ten percent simple interest per annum, that equates to 3.912 minutes.

(60 minutes x .000274 per day for daily interest is .0164 minutes per day. Multiplied by 238 days, = 3.912 minutes.)

Let's just round that up to 4. The way I see it, the government owes me 4 minutes in interest as of tomorrow morning, so, at the appointed hour, instead of setting my clock back to 1:00 a.m., I am going to change my clock from 2:00 a.m. to 12:56 a.m.

In the 1940s, the world was in flames. During this time, we taught our children what fascism was and what it stood for, so that they would understand its evils. The brutal dictatorships of fascism led by Hitler, Mussolini and Franco enslaved, imprisoned, tortured and murdered millions. Nobody really knows the exact number of people who were killed as the forces of fascism attempted to advance their social, political and economic agendas. By the end of that decade, however, they were finally defeated by the forces of liberty. But, in liberty's victory, we came to believe that since we had defeated the evil, we no longer needed to face it. So, in the decades since, we failed to teach our children about the evils inherent in that system. Oh, we told them that fascism is *"bad"* but we did not teach them what it entails. Some, do not remember themselves. Today, there are those that call for the implementation of certain policies not even recognizing that the policies they espouse are at their core fascist in nature; not recognizing the dangers in those policies. The calls to censor political speech through violence, if necessary; and to *"re-educate"* those with whom we disagree into the *"proper way of thinking"* are reminiscent of the very calls made in the 1930s and 1940s. But we have forgotten; and because we have forgotten, because we failed to teach our children, they and we do not see the evil that threatens to engulf us.

But a rose, by any other name still has its thorns.

The 1960s through the 1980s saw the march of communism/socialism across the globe. During this time, we taught our children what communism was and what it stood for, so that they would understand its evils. The forces of liberty faced this threat in a global *"Cold War."* The brutal dictatorships in the Soviet Union, East Germany, Czechoslovakia, Romania, and so many other places imprisoned, tortured and murdered millions. Nobody really knows the exact number of people who were killed as the forces of communism attempted to advance their social, political, and economic agendas. By the 1990s, global communism was finally defeated by the forces of liberty. But, in liberty's victory, we came to believe that since we had defeated the evil, we no longer needed to face it. So, in the decades since, we failed to teach our children about the evils inherent in communism. Oh, we tell our children that communism is *"bad"* but we do not teach them what it entails. Today, there are those that call for the implementation of certain policies — not even recognizing that the policies they espouse are at their heart communist in nature; not recognizing the dangers in those policies. The calls to censor political speech through violence, if necessary; and to *"re-educate"* those with whom we disagree into the *"proper way of thinking"* are so reminiscent of the very calls made in the 1960s through the 1980s. But we have forgotten; and because we have forgotten, because we failed to teach our children, they, and we, do not see the evil that threatens to engulf us.

Why do so many of our youth embrace the policies of fascism? Is it because we failed to teach them how to recognize that threat? They think they know, but then engage in the very actions that are in and of themselves fascist in nature.

Why do so many of our youth embrace the policies of communism/socialism? Is it because we failed to teach them how to recognize that threat? They think they know, but then engage in the very actions that are in and of themselves also fascist in nature.

Did we fail to teach them that fascism and communism, in so many ways, are one and the same? After all, a rose, by any other name, still has its thorns.

And, I wonder, how many roses do we see without recognizing the thorns?

November 11, 2017

Way back when the world was young and God was still a wee boy . . .

While I was in high school, there was this very pretty and smart girl. She was the sweetest and nicest girl imaginable. For some reason that even today some thirty-odd years later I do not know, someone alleged, then spread a rumor, that this girl had slept with the entire football team. Of course, she vociferously denied the allegation. The fact of the matter is that she was a virgin until college. But that fact does not matter. Her denials at the time, well, they did not matter. It is unfortunate that the allegation sullied the girl's reputation. She was so distraught that she left that high school for another. The rumor was so much more delicious than the facts and it spread like wildfire such that in time, everyone believed the rumor to be true. Her denials be damned. The facts be damned.

While I was in college, there was a guy who was accused of sexually assaulting a girl on campus. He vociferously denied the allegation. The fact of the matter is that the girl was jealous because he would not go out with her. She later admitted that her charges were untrue. But that fact does not matter. His denials at the time, well, they did not matter. It is unfortunate that the allegation sullied the boy's reputation. He was so distraught that he left that college for another. You see, the rumor was so much more delicious than the facts that it spread like wildfire such that in time, everyone believed the rumor to be true. His denials be damned. The facts be damned.

Today, I see so many allegations against so many people that, like these rumors, are spread on social media, on television and in print. The rumor spreads like wildfire. Denials do not matter. Facts do not matter. And too often, unproven allegations forever sully one's reputation. But the rumor is so much more delicious than the facts that it spreads and is repeated so often that in time, everyone believes it to be true. Denials be damned. Facts be damned.

Sometimes, allegations and rumors are true. Sometimes, they are not. But in the telling and the retelling, rarely do the denials or the facts matter.

The truth be damned.

NOVEMBER 11, 2017

The needs of a man are few.

The wants of a man are many.

In order to live, a man needs shelter from the elements and food in his belly. Everything else is a thing he wants.

I saw something online this morning that was so funny it made me laugh out loud. But in examining my response, I came to realize that, while it was funny, it was not comedy. It was snarky and mean-spirited. Sure, it made me laugh, but afterward, I felt no joy.

You see, comedy comes from a place of joy. It makes one laugh out of happiness and uplifts him. But there are also many "*funny*" things that come from a darker place — a place of cynicism. One laughs at these snarky comments, they are funny after all, but the cynicism from which they spring is damaging to the soul and uplifts no one. Each time a man laughs out of cynicism, he loses a little bit of his soul.

I saw something snarky online this morning that was so funny it made me laugh out loud, but afterward, I cried.

According to news reports, Charles Manson has passed away.

Manson was the leader of the so-called *"Helter Skelter"* gang. In 1969, he and his cult were charged with horrific murders that were done in an attempt to precipitate a race war of apocalyptic proportion. He is often famously quoted as saying during his trial *"I am the devil."* The horrific murders that he master-minded have been the stuff of legend for the last half century. There is no doubt that this man was pure evil.

While there are those out there that rejoice at his death, I, for one, cannot. While I take comfort in the knowledge that this evil is gone, I take no pleasure in this man's passing. The death of any man, no matter how vile, is nothing to rejoice. Rather, it is perhaps something on which we should reflect.

Manson was a vile human being whose heart was filled with hate and one who had no consideration for his fellow man. But in rejoicing over his death, are we any different? Do our actions today forestall the continuation of his evil or do the anger and hatred we so often display toward each other move us further along the path toward *"Helter Skelter"*?

NOVEMBER 29, 2017

Balance is important.

We have all been to that nice restaurant. You know the one — great food, great service, nice atmosphere, but, when you sit down at the table, it wobbles. One leg or the other is too short or too high. It is very annoying to sit at this unbalanced table. So, you call the waiter over and he applies some temporary fix — a matchbook or napkin under the offending leg — in the hopes that will resolve the problem. Of course, it never really does. That one little annoyance can sometimes make the entire experience unpleasant. Sounds petty, I know, but, that is the truth of the situation.

Of course, a wobbly table is one thing. If the offending leg is so short or so tall that the table actually leans too far, drinks and even food can fall of the table. This will ruin the entire meal and cause one to reconsider going to that restaurant.

Society is like that restaurant and people are like that table. We are built on four legs: body, heart, mind and soul. Too much heart (emotion) or too much body (physicality) unbalances the table. If just one of those legs is even a wee bit out of balance, it makes for an unpleasant situation. If completely out of balance, it can ruin a life or cause one to reconsider their place in that society.

It seems lately that there is way too much heart, way too much feeling in our discourse and not enough mind, not enough thinking.

Is it any wonder that the table is unbalanced? Is it any wonder that the experience is unpleasant?

Maybe it's just me, but I don't understand the furor and consternation by so many about the President's decision to move the US embassy from Tel Aviv to Jerusalem and to recognize Jerusalem as the capital of Israel. Don't misunderstand me. I realize the broader implications of the decision and I understand why people may not believe it is a good idea. I am not opining on the merits of the decision *per se.*

But . . .

As I understand it, in 1995, Congress passed a resolution that called for the embassy to be moved to Jerusalem and for the United States to recognize Jerusalem as Israel's capital. That resolution contained a waiver provision that allowed the president to delay its implementation each and every six months. When passed, it was passed by a 95-3 vote in the Senate. Many of those who voted in favor of that resolution are now excoriating the president for by abiding by its terms.

Each president since the passing of that resolution (Bill Clinton, George W. Bush and Barack Obama) have chosen

345

to invoke the waiver provision and delay the move. In fact, early in his presidency, Donald Trump also invoked that waiver provision. Yesterday, however, Donald Trump decided not to do so, and to allow the resolution to take effect. This morning (and last night), I have heard all of the pundits on television discussing how terrible it was that Mr. Trump did this.

I am utterly confused. Is it terrible that a sitting President chooses to allow a resolution duly passed and enacted by the legislative branch to take effect?

Maybe it's just me, but I thought that the role of the legislature was to pass legislation and the role of the executive was to execute that legislation. But it seems that more and more often there are those among us who want the executive to ignore legislation they do not like, and to enforce only that legislation with which they agree.

Should the president (whomever he may be) be given the authority to ignore laws he does not like and to refuse to enforce those same laws?

How is that different from any dictatorship?

Reps. John Lewis, a civil rights icon, and Bennie Thompson said Thursday they will not attend the opening of the long-awaited civil rights museum in Mississippi. Why? Because President Trump will be there, and they viewed his attendance as an *"insult."*

Many, many years ago, a friend of mine had reached a milestone in her career. So, we decided to throw a fête in her honor. It was going to be a lavish affair and I invited everyone she knew to help her celebrate this accomplishment.

However, two of the invitees, mutual friends of the honoree and myself, did not get along. They hated each other. The reason escapes me, but is irrelevant. Each said that if the other was coming to the celebration, they would not attend. I was left in a quandary — if I invited one the other would not come. What to do?

I invited each. If one chose not to attend and honor their mutual friend, then that only made that person look petty and childish.

I read a very interesting article on civil discourse. The premise of the article was that social media is harming the public. This is something that my partner and I have been discussing much recently.

Does social media harm the public?

My thoughts follow:

The hammer is a very useful tool, but it makes no independent judgment or assessment. It does nothing on its own. The utility of that tool is in the hand of the one that wields it. Used properly, it can be used to build a structure that is bound and strong. But improperly used, it can crush a man's skull.

Social media is a very useful tool, but it makes no independent judgment or assessment. It does nothing on its own. The utility of that tool is in the hand of the one that wields it. Used properly, it can be used to build a structure that is bound and strong. But improperly used, it can crush a man's soul.

No tool is *"ripping apart the social fabric of how society works."*

We are.

All I am saying is that the first three letters of the word diet are D I E.

In the spring of 1692, a group of young girls in Salem Village, Massachusetts, after having claimed to have been possessed by the devil, accused several woman of witchcraft. This ushered in a period of hysteria throughout the colony and a special court was convened to hear the cases. Women were found guilty on little or scant evidence. Often, those accused were accused over perceived slights against the accuser, or for economic or other reasons. In fact, it was impossible to defend against the accusation. Once the accusation was made, it was incumbent upon the accused to prove that she was not a witch. One method of proving innocence was to weigh down the "*witch*" in water. If she floated, she was a witch. If she did not float, she was innocent. Of course, the innocent woman drowned in the process.

In 1787, the newly founded United States adopted its Constitution. Enshrined in that document was the idea of presumption of innocence. I am certain that this was done, in part, because of the excesses of those trials some one-hundred years before. The judicial concept of presumption of innocence was meant to protect men and women from the consequences of mere accusation — to ensure that mere accusation of a crime (like witchcraft) was insufficient to prove such a crime. It was the responsibility of the state to prove that the crime was actually committed. This lifted the burden of defense from the accused and placed the burden of proof where it rightfully belonged; on the accuser.

Fast forward some two-hundred years. Each morning I wake to read or see new accusations of sexual harassment against some politician, celebrity, or other person. The accused loses his job and livelihood. In the court of public opinion, he is adjudged guilty of the crime on no evidence other than mere allegation/accusation. That is not to say that some of these men did not engage in the actions of which they are accused, but the presumption of innocence appears to have been lost. A person's life is ruined by nothing more than mere allegation.

I wonder . . . how many innocents must drown before we catch the witch?

DECEMBER 19, 2017

Everything is relative:

When everything is urgent, nothing is.

When everything is an emergency, nothing is.

When everything is a disaster, nothing is.

December 21, 2017

Today marks the first day of winter. At 11:27 a.m. (EST), the North Pole will be tilted farthest away from the sun ushering in the longest night of the year for the Northern Hemisphere.

In Central Texas, the sun rose at 7:25 a.m. and will set at 5:36 p.m. Where I live, there is a ten percent chance of rain. Temperatures are expected to range between sixty-five degrees and seventy-six degrees. It hardly feels like winter, but this coming weekend we are expected to drop below freezing and the next couple of months are likely to see colder temperatures as Gaia prepares for her rebirth on or about March 20.

For many species, this is the time of hibernation — a winter repose. And much of the surrounding flora will lie dormant as the earth continues its slow revolution around the sun.

For us, perhaps, this is the time to rest and to reflect on the past year and maybe, after this reflection, we can set our dreams and hopes for the upcoming rebirth. Perhaps this is the time for each of us to resolve to be nicer toward each other; to treat each other with respect and dignity; to love each other as we are meant to do; to be better people.

December 30, 2017

It is that time of year again; that time when we all make a resolutions to do this thing or that. Most of us will likely fail. It is not that we do not intend to succeed, rather, it is because change is difficult and it is so easy to fall back into the old patterns we have always maintained.

So this year, my resolutions are modest. I am not going to resolve to lose thirty pounds, to quit smoking or drinking, to save x amount of money or give x amount to charity.

Instead . . .

I will resolve to be healthier with my body; to weigh less, to smoke less, to drink less, and to exercise more. By the end of the year, I won't have a rocking bod and I will still be smoking and drinking, but I will do better.

I will resolve to be kinder in my heart. I won't love everybody. But I will be just a little bit nicer. I will make one less snarky remark to someone. By the end of the year, I won't be the most loving and kindest person in the world, but I will do better.

I will resolve to be more thoughtful in my mind; to read one more book; to learn one more new thing; to try one more different thing that I have not tried before. By the end of the year, I won't be any smarter or wiser, but I will do better.

I will resolve to be more accepting in my soul; to be thankful for the little things and to not let other things bring me down; to accept the blessing of Providence without asking why it wasn't exactly what I wanted. By the end of the year, I won't be a saint, but I will do better.

My resolution is simply that by the end of 2018, I will have done better. I will be better.

JANUARY 11, 2018

Painting people with a broad brush based on race, creed, color, national origin, gender or sexual orientation is bigoted — regardless of which race, creed, color, national origin, gender or sexual orientation is being painted.

JANUARY 11, 2018

You Can't Stop Progress

Way back when I was young and God was still a wee boy
. . .

I recall using a manual typewriter for my research and term papers. I loved this tool. It was so much nicer and better than writing it all out long-hand. In time, that tool was replaced by the IBM Selectric – an electric typewriter that had more bells and whistles and made writing that much easier. Those were simpler times.

Eventually, even that was replaced by a word processor and finally, the computer. There were those who were concerned that the typewriter repairmen would no longer be able to find jobs, but the jobs evolved into something else. I wonder, does anyone use typewriters anymore?

I recall going to the gas station to fill up my car's tank. As I drove across the bell hose it dinged announcing my arrival to the attendant in the station. (Fifty-three cents a gallon! Outrageous! I thought.) The attendant duly came out, pumped my gas, checked my tire pressure and the oil level under the hood. He washed my windows and took my payment. Over time, that full-service was replaced with self-service pumps. Those were simpler times.

Today, I get out of my car, pump my own gas, wash my own windows, check my own tire pressure and oil levels. (But only when the computer in the car tells me there may be a problem.) As these self-serve pumps replaced full-service stations, there were those who were concerned that the attendants would no longer be able to find jobs, but the jobs evolved into something else. I wonder, does anyone use full-service anymore?

I recall going to the bank and waiting in line each and every Friday to withdraw money for the weekend. I had to cash a check to do this. Sometimes, if I was unable to make it to the bank, I could go to the grocery store and cash a check there for an amount over my purchase (cash back, they called it). Those were simpler times.

Today, bank tellers and grocery store check cashing has been supplanted by ATM's, and there were those who were concerned that the tellers and clerks would no longer be able to find jobs, but the jobs evolved into something else. I wonder, does anyone use checks anymore?

Today, in most fast-food restaurants, one goes into the establishment, pays a cashier and is given his food. But change is coming and increasingly we see self-pay kiosks sprouting forth in these establishments. When our children recall their youth, they will marvel at these simpler times.

Recently, I have seen many on social media expressing angst and consternation at the possibility of cashier-less fast-food establishments, but, the bottom line is that we cannot stop progress. Things will change whether we are prepared for the change or not. Angst and consternation over these changes will not stop them.

In the not-too-distant future, the fast-food cashier will no longer exist. The jobs that are lost as a result will have evolved into something else. And, our children will wonder whether anyone ever hands cash to people anymore.

January 15, 2018

I never ceased to be amazed by the cognitive dissonance of those who wear ideological blinders. While it is, generally, a good thing that the American people are a forgiving lot, increasingly, that forgiveness is only extended to those with whom we agree.

For example:

In 1990, then Mayor of Washington DC, Marion Barry was arrested when he was caught on camera smoking crack with a prostitute. He was found guilty and later sentenced to six months in federal prison. Two months after his release from prison in 1992, he ran for (and won) a seat on the DC Council. Later, he ran for (and won) his fourth term as mayor. Those who opposed him ideologically condemned him. But for those who supported him, criminal convictions did not matter.

In 2017, former Sheriff Joe Arpaio was convicted of defying a court order (criminal contempt). He was pardoned by Donald Trump. Now he is running for Senate. Those who oppose him ideologically condemn him. But for those who support him, criminal convictions do not matter.

In 2013, Chelsea Manning (then Bradley Edward Manning) was convicted by court-martial of violating the Espionage Act. After the sentence was commuted by then-President Barack Obama, Manning was released from Fort Leavenworth in 2017. Now, she has announced her intent to run for Senate from the state of Maryland. Those who oppose her ideologically condemn her. But for those who support her, criminal convictions do not matter.

In American politics today, one is condemned by those who oppose him ideologically, but for those who support him, criminal convictions do not matter.

In American politics today, it seems that, it does not matter if one is right or wrong, it only matters what side he's on.

January 17, 2018

I watched portions of the news conference yesterday about the President's medical exam. The media was in a huge uproar complaining that the President is:

1) on cholesterol medications;

2) borderline obese; and,

3) eats too much fast food and doesn't exercise.

I am not sure what their complaints are about.

According to the Centers for Disease Control, in 2011 – 2012 thirty-seven percent (37%) of Americans had cholesterol issues. (See, https://www.cdc.gov/cholesterol/facts.htm.)

Twenty-eight percent (28%) of Americans over age 40 are taking cholesterol medication. (See, https://www.acsh.org/news/2015/12/04/cdc-study-reveals-that-too-few-americans-are-on-statins)

Almost thirty-eight percent (37.9%) of adults over age twenty (20) are obese. (See,

https://www.cdc.gov/nchs/fastats/obesity-
overweight.htm)

According to the Huffington Post, eight out of ten
Americans eat fast food at least once a month. (See,
https://www.huffingtonpost.com/2013/08/06/fast-food-
poll_n_3714988.html)

According to CBS news, eighty percent (80%) of
Americans do not get the recommended amount of
exercise. (See, https://www.cbsnews.com/news/cdc-80-
percent-of-american-adults-dont-get-recommended-
exercise/)

So, what is the media's complaint? Is it that this
representative of the American people is representative of
the American people?

January 20, 2018

The biggest threat to American democracy is the political party system. It does not seem to matter whether the candidate has a (D) or an (R) after his name. They are the same. They are interested only in party politics and in gaining and maintaining power. Neither of these parties seem interested in addressing the issues of the American people.

Maybe, going forward, we should each vote third-party. It does not matter which one, because the goal would not be to take control of Congress.

Maybe if the American people deny the majority of Congressional seats to each of these two main parties, then they will be forced to reach a compromise of some sort. They will have no choice, but to work with each other (or one of the other parties) to deal with the people's business. There will be no alternative for them, but to cooperate, compromise and work with others.

Maybe by denying either of these two main parties the majority, they will be unable to continue to play political games, engage in partisanship and accrue more power for themselves.

It is time for a new American Revolution — one brought forth at the ballot box where, we the American people, stand up and say, *"Enough is enough"* and finally, throw the bums out.

January 20, 2018

On the article about the man who attacked Rand Paul and broke his ribs. The reason stated in this article is that Rand Paul, while mowing his lawn, stacked brush on his own property, but "*near*" the property line of his attacker.

I don't know which is more disgusting. The idea that Paul may have been attacked over political beliefs or that he was attacked over such a ridiculous reason.

Have we really gotten to a place in our society where we believe that resorting to this kind of violence to settle disputes is acceptable?

Having the right to do a thing, should not be confused with doing the right thing.

I cannot be the only one who finds it odd that:

There are those among us who would protest against police departments and their alleged abuse of power, while others proclaim that such protests are undermining American law enforcement.

Concurrently,

There are those among us who would protest against the FBI and their abuse of power, while others proclaim that such protests are undermining American law enforcement.

Whether one stands in protest or in support of the law enforcement agency, depends entirely on what side of the political aisle one stands and which law enforcement agency they support.

It doesn't matter if its right or wrong. It only matters what side you're on.

To have knowledge of an event before it occurs (pre-knowledge) is to be prescient.

To judge something before it occurs (pre-judgment) is to be prejudiced.

If one believes the reports, the far left hates Donald Trump's immigration proposal.

If one believes the reports, the far right hates Donald Trump's immigration proposal.

I believe that's called compromise.

There are extreme forces in our society that believe any compromise with the opposition is a bad thing. In fact, they view the opposition not as people who may have a differing viewpoint, but rather as the enemy, because they do not support their ideals and/or principles.

But in a diverse society it is necessary to embrace and accept differences; to come to compromise on those ideas that seem so diametrically opposed to each other. In truth, compromise is the bedrock of democracy.

To those who are so adamantly opposed to compromise, I have to ask: Why are you opposed to democracy?

Someone once wrote a post that offered to correct my *"grammer"*.

I said, "Ok, as long as I can correct your spelling."

FEBRUARY 10, 2018

I read an article yesterday that a school district in Minnesota was banning the books *"Huckleberry Finn"* and *"To Kill A Mockingbird"* from their curriculum. These books contained certain words that are deemed offensive. The school district believes that it can teach the same lesson contained in these books by using different works of literature.

As a writer, I don't much cotton to that idea. There is a reason that these two books are considered American classics. The idea, the story, that is told is done so in a way to provoke thought by the reader. The use of certain offensive or pejorative words and phrases is not done so for simple gratuity. The use of those words and phrases, especially when done in a such a casual manner, is meant to evoke thought and consideration and to place context as to the time and place.

If we remove offensive words from historical works, are we not removing the context necessary for the story to unfold? For example, in a story about the underpinnings racism, how is one to truly understand that underlying

376

racism if the "*n word*" is suddenly erased from its historical context within the pages of that book? The word itself is, in fact, offensive, but it was also, in fact, routinely used at certain times and in certain places. If we remove that word from books that describe those times and places, are we not also removing prime exemplars of the nature of the racism that the book warns against? By doing so, we are altering the story, such that, the story itself becomes invalid. If we remove books from circulation that contain such offensive words, how are we to enable readers to truly understand how ubiquitous the offensive behavior was? We become all consumed about the offense of a single word, that we lose sight of the context of the entirety of the story. We cannot see the forest because of a single tree.

I read that news article and was immediately reminded of Orwell's "*1984.*" Here is a book whose themes included the control of language as a means of controlling a population. First, control the language, then control the thought, and, finally, the thought-process itself.

The article saddened me and I began to wonder how long it would be before that school district decides to ban Bradbury's "*Fahrenheit 451*" and whether the district would even recognize the irony of doing so.

Once again, a horrific tragedy unfolds in one of our nation's schools and the lives of seventeen people are cut short by a criminal perpetrator intent on violence. Collectively, we shake our heads and ask, "*Why?*" Almost immediately after the event, the finger pointing begins:

Some say that the problem is guns, and that guns should be banned altogether.

Some say that the problem is a failure of background checks that allow those with mental illness to obtain these weapons.

Some say that the problem is lack of security in our schools.

Some say that the problem lies with a government that is too paralyzed to solve the problem.

Some blame white supremacists.

Some blame a hyper-masculine culture.

Some blame identity politics.

Some blame the President; some blame Congress.

The left blames the right, the right blames left; democrats blame republicans, republicans blame democrats; whites blame Hispanics who blame African-Americans who blame Asians who blame Muslims who blame Jews who blame Christians who blame . . .

Collectively, we shake our heads and ask, "*Why?*"

We celebrate violence with our children:

In their video games (consider *Mortal Kombat, Grand Theft Auto*).

In their movies (consider Jason Bourne movies, *John Wick, Kill Bill*).

In their television shows (consider *Lethal Weapon, SWAT, 9-1-1*).

By our comedians (Kathy Griffith holding up a severed head of the president, Rosie O'Donnell calling for a military coup.)

By riots after football games that we call "*celebrations.*"

By riots on college campuses held because we cannot bear to hear opposing points of view.

By hanging effigies of presidents to be beaten by sticks (*pinatas*).

- Collectively, we shake our heads and ask, "*Why?*"

- We celebrate hate:

- In social media posts that "*despise*" anyone who disagrees with them.

- In commentary that calls another with whom we disagree "*racists, bigots, misogynists*", etc.

379

- By making up derogatory words (*repugs, libtards*).

Collectively, we shake our heads and ask, "*Why?*"

We teach our children that it is ok to hate.

We teach our children that violence is ok.

Collectively, we shake our heads and ask, "*Why?*" Almost immediately after the event, the finger pointing begins. Yet the finger is never pointed where it needs to be — at the mirror.

February 17 2018

I read the Mueller indictment and a few articles about it. The indictment is against thirteen Russian individuals and three Russian organizations and outlines how these individuals and organizations worked to disrupt the elections by sowing discord among the American electorate. According to the report, these provocateurs actively worked to disparage Hillary Clinton, Marco Rubio and Ted Cruz. The goal was to discredit any candidate they believed to be anti-Russian. They also worked to enhance the candidacies of Donald Trump, Jill Stein and Bernie Sanders. They were not trying to support one candidate over another. According to the indictment, the goal was to sow the seeds of discord by promoting or denigrating various candidates.

After the election, they organized rallies **against** Donald Trump (and likely continue to do so). This was not to support his political opponents, but to rather to oppose him. The purpose, or so it seems, was not to support or oppose anyone, but rather to fuel the fires of anger and hatred.

The indictment even prompted a tweet by the Brookings Institute that purports to quote Sergey Aleksasheko (a nonresident Senior Fellow for Global Economy and Development at the Institute) to say: *"In the 2016 election, Putin was not looking for Trump to win, he was looking to destabilize the American political situation. He did it. It does not matter who won, he destabilized Washington completely. That was his achievement. He will do it again in 2018."* (See, https://twitter.com/BrookingsInst/status/96457964453939 2000_)

However, I take issue with Aleksasheko's assessment.

You see, it does not really matter how many political ads a foreign government may have purchased. Nor does it really matter how many so-called fake news stories they may have disseminated. It does not matter how many political rallies may have been organized. Those activities in and of themselves did not *"destabilize Washington."* Those actions did not sow discord in the American electorate.

The fact is, it was not Russian provocateurs who posted statements like:

"Anyone who supports Trump is a racist, bigot, misogynist, homophobe, ignorant or just plain stupid." That was posted by an American citizen.

*"Hillary Clinton is a crook and a b****."* That was posted by an American citizen.

*"Republicans are f****** idiots."* That was posted by an American citizen.

"The democrats are a bunch of cry-babies." That was posted by an American citizen.

"I despise Trump and anyone who supported him." That was posted by an American citizen.

While it may be true that Russian provocateurs watered the seeds of discord, those seeds had long ago been planted in fertile ground.

Neither the Russians nor Putin are to blame for destabilizing the American political situation. Neither the Russians nor Putin are to blame for the discord in the political system. That responsibility falls with the American citizenry.

When we resort to such attacks on each other, **we** sow the discord. When we refer to other Americans in such a manner, **we** destabilize the American system. When we misbehave, **we** are the cause of the division in our society.

If we cannot rise above petty politics and remember that we are each and every one of us Americans first, and work together, we sow the seeds of discord and are responsible for the destabilization of our own country.

Neither the Russians nor Putin can exploit us, if we do not allow them to do so.

No foreign government should ever interfere in the electoral process of another nation.

Founded in 1950, Radio Free Europe broadcast into Eastern Europe. It was funded by the US Government. Its goal was to influence the people in Eastern Europe to rid themselves of their communist regimes and move toward a more democratic model. (See, https://pressroom.rferl.org/p/6092.html)

In the early 1980s, the US government created a similar system aimed at the communist regime in Cuba. It was eventually named Radio Marti. Its goal was to influence the Cuban people to oust their communist government. (See, https://en.wikipedia.org/wiki/Radio_y_Televisión_Mart%C3%AD)

In the 2000s , President Obama warned that the UK would be at the *"back of the queue"* in any trade deal if they chose to leave the EU. Many Brits condemned this as a blatant attempt to interfere with the UK's Brexit vote. (See, https://www.theguardian.com/politics/2016/apr/22/barack-obama-brexit-uk-back-of-queue-for-trade-talks)

Also in the 2000s, the Obama State Department paid hundreds of thousands of taxpayer dollars to an Israeli group who used that money in a campaign to defeat Israeli Prime Minister Netanyahu in favor of another candidate. (See, https://www.washingtontimes.com/news/2016/jul/12/obama-admin-sent-taxpayer-money-oust-netanyahu/)

Like many Americans, I decry Russian meddling in our electoral process and strongly believe that we should do whatever we can to mitigate any such interference. But let's not kid ourselves here. We are just as guilty of interference.

No foreign government should ever interfere in the electoral process of another nation. But those in glass houses, should not cast stones.

According to IMDB, the movie *"Minority Report"* (2002, starring Tom Cruise) was set in a future where " . . . a *special police unit is able to arrest murderers before they commit their crimes, an officer from that unit is himself accused of a future murder."*

This movie warned against the abrogation of Constitutional rights based upon a belief that a person had the propensity to commit a crime. These so-called precriminals were arrested and prosecuted before they had the opportunity to commit their crime. Of course, supporters of the program said that this was done in order to protect the public from a future murder that may be committed. The title, *"Minority Report"* is a reference to the possibility that the so-called crime may not actually occur. After all, in any future, there are paths that may be taken that change that future. Still, people were arrested for *"pre-crime."*

As I read some of the essays about issues facing our society today that support the notion that we must do more to prevent criminal acts, including, and up to, the denial of Constitutional rights to those who **may** engage in such an act, I cannot help but wonder . . . are we denying rights to people based on a belief that a crime may occur as opposed to one that actually does?

Are we ignoring the Minority Report?

The human animal is an amazing creature whose capacity to create is only surpassed by its capacity to destroy.

February 22, 2018

In the old Soviet Union, private ownership of property was illegal. The communist regime told its people that all goods were owned by the State and those who were against giving up private ownership were unpatriotic.

In the United States today, there are those who say that if one does not wish to pay higher taxes (giving up private ownership to the State) then that person is unpatriotic.

Silly, me; I thought we had won the Cold War.

Mario Kiefer

February 22, 2018

I love reading horror stories about monsters. Each of the stories seem to have a common theme in that, regardless of the type of monster, it is generally impervious to force. Only by starving the monster can one destroy it. The werewolf cannot be killed by bullets or blades, but if one denies it meat, it will starve. The vampire is likewise impervious to weapons, but if one denies it blood, it will starve. All monsters starve when denied the sustenance needed to live.

The federal government is a bloated monster that feeds on tax payer dollars. The only way to stop this monster is to starve it.

FEBRUARY 22, 2018

So, they are talking about raising the legal age to purchase a gun to twenty-one. I don't have a problem with that *per se*, but . . .

At what age do Americans reach adulthood and should any rights be denied to an adult citizen?

We can drive at sixteen.

We can vote at eighteen.

We can die for our country at eighteen.

We cannot drink until we are twenty-one.

We can stay on our parent's insurance until we are twenty-six.

We cannot rent a car until we are twenty-six.

If one is an adult, than one should be afforded all the privileges that come with adulthood. If one is an adult, than one should have all the responsibilities of adulthood.

There are federal laws on the books related to the regulation of marijuana. Some states have chosen to pass laws in contradiction to those federal laws, have refused to enforce those federal laws and have actively worked to thwart them. Many say that is a good thing.

There are federal laws on the books related to the regulation of immigration. Some states have chosen to pass laws in contradiction to those federal laws, have refused to enforce those federal laws and have actively worked to thwart them. Many say that is a good thing.

So, I guess that if the US Congress passes federal laws related to the regulation of assault rifles, states will be able to pass laws in contradiction to that federal law, refuse to enforce that federal law and actively work to thwart it. I am sure that those who support the state's rights in the first two examples, will support the state's rights in the latter and say that is a good thing.

MARCH 2, 2018

Way back when the world was young and God was still a wee boy . . .

I got my first "real job." It was for a small, solo practitioner who focused on criminal defense, workers' compensation and probate matters (conservatorships and guardianships) along with the occasional personal injury work. There were only three of us in that office, in addition to a contract attorney who occasionally attended depositions or hearings on our behalf — generally due to scheduling conflicts. We had two computers in the office that were not networked. We exchanged files on a single-sided 3½-inch floppy disk, but with 400 KB formatted capacity. Research was done in the library. Communications were either in person, on the phone or by fax. It seemed like such a waste of time when we considered how many minutes of the day were wasted just trying to communicate. Still, we thought we were so efficient, even if we longed for an easier, less time-consuming way to do so.

My next job was for a small plaintiff's firm. This time, we had a network of computers. We exchanged files by saving them to a central location on that network. Research was still done in the library and communications continued to be in person, on the phone or by fax. But, now, we didn't have to exchange those disks. We were able to access whatever document we needed right there on our computer! Sometimes, when we had a quick question but could not get the person with the answer on the phone, we had to hunt them down throughout the office in order to vet out that answer. It seemed like such a waste of time when we considered how many tenths of an hour of the day was wasted just trying to communicate. Still, we thought we were so efficient, even if we longed for an easier, less time-consuming way to do so.

When I took my next position it was with a firm that specialized in toxic tort defense. Here we actually had a lone computer that could connect to Lexis (across one of those telephone line modems that made the horrible screeching sound each time one tried to connect). The costs were, of course, outrageous. We even had a database that allowed us to track our cases. Finally, we had something called "ccmail." Of course, this only connected us internally to others within the office and trying to communicate externally (leaving messages and waiting for return calls) was agonizing. It seemed like such a waste of time when we considered how many quarters of an hour of the day was wasted just trying to communicate. Still, we thought we were so efficient, even if we longed for an easier, less time-consuming way to do so.

A few years later and 2,000 miles away, I took a job with a firm that was years ahead in technology. I was issued a laptop that could connect (over the phone line, still using that horrible dial-up modem) into the office. Files were still stored in a central location on the network, but now, I could access them even from the comfort of my hotel when traveling. We had email, calling a person on the telephone seemed like such a waste of time. Many of our outside contacts still did not have email, so in order to exchange documents with them, we had to use the fax machine. It seemed like such a waste of time when we considered how many halves of an hour of the day was wasted just trying to communicate. Still, we thought we were so efficient, even if we longed for an easier, less time-consuming way to do so.

Time and technology has certainly progressed since those days. Today, we save documents to a document management system that indexes them; and we can access those files from anywhere in the world through a secure remote system. We still have the occasional in-person meetings and telephone calls (sometimes too many to count!), but email has supplanted most of that as the primary form of communication. We don't use fax machines anymore. Why fax something when you can simply image your document in a PDF format and exchange it over email (or send it over in its native format, if you prefer). Documents are served and filed through secure websites set up by the courts (or in some jurisdictions, vendors authorized by those courts).

Each morning, we pour through tens (if not hundreds) of email that came in the night before, sometime spending significant amounts of time just reviewing, organizing and determining what's important.

And when I consider the number of hours spent reviewing those email, I wonder, are we being more efficient? Is there an easier and less time-consuming way to communicate? Perhaps, in-person, by telephone or via fax?

MARCH 5, 2018

Amazing how many manage to look down on others when they do not hold the high ground.

MARCH 6, 2018

I voted today and I encourage everyone to do so. I don't care how you vote, but before you do, please read about and understand who or what you are voting on. Voting for the mere sake of voting without having an understanding of the issues serves no purpose. American democracy is dependent upon an informed electorate.

Get informed. Then go vote.

MARCH 17, 2018

The Optimist sees the glass as half-full.

The Pessimist sees the glass as half-empty.

The Cynic knows that one is going to throw the contents in the other's face.

March 18, 2018

In 2008, the American taxpayer coughed up nearly a trillion dollars for "*shovel ready jobs*" that were meant to "*fix America's failing infrastructure.*" Yet, the infrastructure has not been fixed.

So in 2018, the politicians are telling the taxpayer that we need to cough up another trillion dollars to "*fix America's failing infrastructure.*" And we ask, where did that past trillion dollars go?

The question is, of course, rhetorical. We know where that money went. It went into the pockets of the friends and supporters of the politicians who were in power at that time. And America's infrastructure still needs to be fixed.

Ten years from now, I predict, the politicians will be telling the American taxpayer that we need to cough up another trillion dollars to "*fix America's failing infrastructure.*" Some of us will ask, where did the money we gave in 2018 go? Of course, the question will be rhetorical. We know where it will go.

And twenty years from now, I predict, we still will need to *"fix America's failing infrastructure."*

MARCH 20, 2018

Today is the first day of spring. Day and night will be balanced. If only we could learn from nature.

Isaac Asimov (January 2, 1920 – April 6, 1992) was a prolific American science fiction writer, probably best known for his *Foundation* series books.

In 1957, Asimov published his book, *"The Naked Sun."* This book focused on a world with a small, controlled population that used robots to perform most tasks. The people of this world lived on large estates and were taught from birth to avoid personal contact. They were expected to be alone or spend time only with their spouses, if they must spend time with anyone at all. Face-to-face contact (called *"seeing"*) was actively discouraged. While it was, sometimes, necessary to *"see"* people, society considered this disgusting, dirty and vulgar.

Instead, people were encouraged and expected to interact through holographic imagery called *"viewing."* Virtually all connections were made through *"viewing."* While *"viewing"* there were little or no rules of modesty or propriety.

As a young man, I thought this idea was preposterous. After all, people would seek out others if for no other reason than sexual relations. Human contact and interaction is necessary and those connections lead to a greater understanding of each other and those connections are, after all, necessary. Especially for those in their young adult years where sex seems to be the singularity upon which their lives revolve.

But today, in reading this book, I sometimes wonder whether Asimov had a crystal ball that allowed him to spy into today's social media. After all, in a society where even sexual contact can be gratified through chance encounters with strangers through apps such as Tindr, Grindr and others, that physical need for sexual fulfillment is abated.

But what about the emotional needs? These are strengthened by physical intimacy with someone one loves.

What about the emotional fulfillment that comes from direct human contact that cannot come from mere "*viewing*"?

As I consider this book today, I wonder if perhaps Asimov's warning in this book was a warning against failing to create meaningful connections that are necessarily derived from human contact.

Of course, it is not lost on me that I write these queries sitting alone in a darkened room as I prepare to post them on that social media

And, I wonder, was Asimov looking into a future mirror that reflects our present day?

I am hearing so much hullabaloo about including a citizenship question on the 2020 Census, that it made me think about what the Constitution actually calls for. In examining that document, the enumeration requirement is provided for under Article I, Section 2.

A plain reading of the that clause states:

"... *Representatives and direct Taxes shall be apportioned among the several States which may be included within this Union, according to their respective Numbers, which shall be determined by adding to the whole Number of free Persons, including those bound to Service for a Term of Years, and excluding Indians not taxed, three-fifths of all other Persons*. . ."

It goes on to provide that the enumeration of persons shall be conducted " . . . *in such Manner as they shall by Law direct.*" The "*they*" here means the US Congress.

To achieve this, the Census Bureau was created by Congress as a part of the US Department of Commerce. The Director of the Census Bureau is appointed by the US President.

The questionnaire that the Bureau provides asks many questions that are irrelevant to the Constitutional requirement. These questions are meant to elicit demographic information that can be used by Congress in determining, among other things, funding need, but, make no mistake, nowhere in the Constitution is the collection of such information required or contemplated. How many people are of what demographic is irrelevant to the enumeration clause except, insofar as the demographics reviewed include *"Indians not taxed"* or are *"free Persons."*

All of the hullabaloo that is currently swirling around the questions on the Census could so easily be avoided if our lawmakers avoided implementing extra-Constitutional requirements and instead, focused solely on their Constitutional mandate, i.e., count the number of people, in accordance with the provisions for that enumeration.

This can be done with one question: Are you a resident of the United States who is a *"free person"* or *"Indian not taxed"*?

Anything else is Constitutionally irrelevant.

APRIL 10, 2018

Simple economics: As long as there are enough people willing to purchase the iPhone X for $1,000, it will sell for $1,000. Only when enough people say, *"I won't pay that much,"* will the price drop.

All the News that's Fit to Print – and even that which is not.

I just watched some "news" reports on a couple of the 24-hour cable news networks that were related to a "raid" on the offices of the President's former doctor and all that I can do is shake my head.

Put aside your feelings for Donald Trump for a moment. It really should not matter whether you like him or not. Close your eyes and put yourself in Mr. Trump's shoes for just the tiniest of moments.

Now, imagine, if you will . . .

For thirty years you have seen the same physician (let's call him Dr. X) but you took a new job in another state, so, now you are seeing a different doctor.

For whatever reason, Dr. X shares your personal medical information with a major newspaper and that paper (whose motto is "*All the News that's Fit to Print*") runs a story detailing your personal medical information for all the world to see. How would you feel? What would your reaction be? What would you do?

Would you go to Dr. X and demand a return of any and every scrap of paper that Dr. X may have on you? Would you want to feel assured that Dr. X no longer has any information about your private condition(s) that s/he could share with others?

Keep your eyes closed and continue to imagine that you are the person whose private medical information was published by a major newspaper. Now, imagine that some other worthy "news" organizations broadcast the story that you demanded a return of your medical records from this doctor. In the process of their broadcasts, they, too, share your private medical details. Of course, they say that they do this in the context of the story about your "raid" on the doctor's office, but if that were their true motivation, then there is no need to share the private medical details, is there? The story can be told without those details. No, clearly, these "news" organizations were simply seeking to embarrass you.

If this were you and not Mr. Trump, you would be outraged by this doctor's behavior and by the behavior of the "news" organizations that chose to share those details.

Shame on the doctor who shared private medical details about a patient (any patient) with the newspaper.

Shame on that newspaper for publishing those details.

Shame on the networks that chose to broadcast those details after the fact.

"*All the News that's Fit to Print*" and even that which is not.

May 2, 2018

I was reading the story about the girl who wore a traditional Chinese dress to the prom. She posted pictures of herself wearing that dress and, naturally, the trolls came out to disparage her.

"That's cultural appropriation!" they cried. *"How dare a white girl wear a traditional Chinese dress!"*

But . . .

Isn't the United States a nation of immigrants? Isn't America a multi-cultural country?

What should the girl wear? What is the appropriate *"American"* attire? If we are, in fact, a multi-cultural nation of immigrants, isn't the *"American"* culture one that embraces the traditions of many cultures, or are we only to embrace the culture of our ethnic origins?

Is it cultural appropriation when a Chinese-American man orders a burrito?

Is it cultural appropriation when a young Hispanic child listens to rap music?

Is it cultural appropriation if an African-American cooks a Japanese dinner at home?

Is it cultural appropriation if a Japanese-American wears a cowboy hat?

The single largest selling condiment in America today is salsa. If a non-Hispanic American buys salsa, is that cultural appropriation?

If, as so many proclaim, the American culture is a rich mix of ancestries and ethnicities — an amalgamation of the cultural roots of the many immigrants that have come to these shores, then isn't a traditional Chinese dress part of the American culture?

And, if that dress is part of the American culture, what's wrong with an American wearing it — regardless of her biological ethnicity?

Yes, it is cultural appropriation. But let's not forget that a multi-cultural society cannot exist without appropriating from the cultures that make it up.

May 25, 2018

It's actually a brilliant strategy.

The power structure has convinced the American people that any given issue is a line, and that we must choose one side of that line or other.

As we each are busy taking our side, we are distracted from the fact that the issue is really a circle that keeps the power structure within, while the people are kept out.

MAY 30, 2018

"A cynical, mercenary, demagogic press will in time produce a people as base as itself." ~ Joseph Pulitzer.

I wonder if Pulitzer is pleased with the awards that bear his name — and the recipients thereof.

June 1, 2018

Those who decry political games want to effect political change.

Those who want to effect political change, must first get elected.

Those who want to get elected, must first play political games.

JUNE 4, 2018

Any work that has the ability to make the viewer root for the bad guy without realizing that he was, in fact, the bad guy, is a fine piece of art.

June 5, 2018

I rise at my usual time — just before six a.m. Like a single-minded zombie (Do zombies have minds?) I stumble from my bedroom to the kitchen (Must have coffee! Must have coffee! Must have coffee!) and turn on the Keurig to warm up. If only these old bones could warm so easily. I thank God that the Keurig is plumbed and I don't have to deal with pouring water into the container. I then stumble through the back door for my morning fix. As the nicotine courses from my lungs into my bloodstream, I feel the first stirrings of wakefulness.

This task now complete, I stumble back to the kitchen (Must have coffee! Must have coffee! Must have coffee!) and pour the first cup of God's elixir. Then, I shuffle to the living room where I plop my fat ass (Yes, it's fat. What of it?) onto the sofa. I pick up the remote — exactly where I left it the night before —— and turn on the television to listen to the talking heads.

First, Spectrum News (Channel No. 1 on my cable provider). Not sure why I need to know what the weather is going to be. It's not as if I am commuting around town today. Reports are that we likely will hit 100 degrees this afternoon. I push the *"up"* button and go through the local channels (2 through 5 on my provider's network). Traffic accidents, weather, local politics, a couple of feel-good stories. Nothing terribly interesting, but good data for the hard drive of my brain. These days, the input is so much easier than the output.

I change the channel to No. 46 — CNN. (*"Trump is evil. Trump is evil. Trump is evil."*)

Then, I move up to No. 47 — HLN shows a little girl running to her daddy who just returned from his military tour overseas. The host says. *"I just cannot get enough of these military reunion videos."* I can.

I move up the channels to No. 48 — FoxNews. (*"Trump is good; God is great; people are crazy."*)

I move on to No. 49 — MSNBC (*"Trump is the devil. Trump is the devil. Trump is the devil."*)

I return to the local channels searching for **news**.

I finish my first cup of go-go juice and walk (no more shuffling) to the kitchen where I start cup no. 2. I may as well go outside for another coffin-nail while I wait for it to brew. Outside, the sun rises and the yard is quiet except for the incessant coo-coo-cooing of the pigeons that have overtaken the trees in the back. I ponder the existence of these rats on wings. Despite their cacophony, I think, *"Life is good."*

I return indoors. In the kitchen, my coffee sings to me like a siren from Greek mythology. She is luring me toward the sweet abyss. (*"Come on,"* she sings. *"You know you want me. You know you cannot live without me. You know that you must have me.*") Unable to resist the melody, dutifully, I obey. I pick up my coffee and return to my perch on the sofa to flip incessantly through channels, up and down, down and up, back and forth, looking for something (anything) that can be called **news**. Why do they call it "*news*" if so much of it is recycled pablum? Should it not be called "*olds*"?

I glance at the clock. It's seven a.m. How did that happen? I just woke up! I bid farewell to the six o'clock hour and turn off the television set. Awake now, I briskly walk outside and strip to my skivvies. Into the pool, I jump and, for the next twenty minutes, I swim . . . back and forth . . . back and forth . . . back and forth.

I climb out of the pool and look down at myself. I cannot believe that I did not lose thirty pounds in the last twenty minutes! Surely, by now I should have the body of a Greek god! Yet, despite all of that swimming, my derriere is still as fat as it was before I started. I towel myself dry, pick up my clothing and go inside.

After a pit stop at the laundry hamper, I start my morning ablutions. Shower, shave, dress and then into my office to start my day. It's a quarter-to-eight.

I turn on my computer and look up my book sales. (Six more yesterday! Yea!) I check for new reviews; none as of yet today.

Now on to social media: That cute guy who has been trolling me on Instagram has posted another shirtless pic. I start to move on, then I figure, what the hell, and click the "*like*" button. Then I consider, could this be the reason my spam folder is filled with so much porn? I click again to un-like.

I am at LinkedIn now. Two more individuals have viewed my most recent post. I glance at the newsfeed, but there is nothing that interests me. (Well, there is that one story about people moving from one state to another, but it's not terribly informative and the comments are, at times, downright nasty.) I see that a recruiter has checked out my profile and sent me a message. *"Not today,"* I think. *"Maybe, tomorrow."* For today, I do not respond.

On to Twitter: I see a couple of feel-good tweets from some people I follow. I look at the *"news."* (Does anyone **really** care what a celebrity thinks? I do not.)

Now, I'm off to Facebook. I see two notifications. Someone in my local *"broadcast"* group asks whether anyone witnessed an accident yesterday. *"Not me,"* I think, and move on.

Another in the *"writer's"* group is looking for beta readers for her latest work. I would do it, but I am in the middle of my next project and simply do not have enough time right now. Suddenly, my deceased mother whispers in my ear: *"There is always time, if you spend your time wisely. It's only a matter of how you choose."* Feeling guilty, now, I respond that I would be happy to review.

My one good eye wanders to the *"trending"* section. There is a large disclaimer: Facebook will be removing this section soon. It seems that section is plagued by fake news. Is it any surprise? When human beings cannot distinguish fact from fiction, can we really expect an algorithm to do so?

I consider posting something, then decide, *"Nah, I really don't have anything say this morning."* The voice of a demon within responds with a chortle: *"You, don't have something to say?!?"*) Then my angelic mother intercedes: *"Not all thoughts should be voiced."* Demon or angel? To whom should I accede? I do not post.

I return to my book sales dashboard. Two more sold this morning. (Woo hoo!) Then back through various news sites (FoxNews, CNN, MSNBC, Statesman, BBC and Al Jazeera. Yeah, yeah, I know. Many say to me, *"How dare you watch this or that network!"*, but, hey, I am well rounded! I actually **like** different points of view. I know that makes me a rare commodity in today's online culture.)

It's now eight forty-five a.m. I exit the social media accounts and turn to my work computer. It's time to start the day.

For the next four hours, I respond to email and voicemail and attend conference call after conference call. I wonder, *"When am I actually supposed to get work done?"*

At the appointed lunch hour. I log out of work. (I really didn't need to be on that last call!) Normally, I would step outside for twenty minutes of swim time, but today, well today, I must have blood work done for my doctor's appointment on the fourteenth. I ponder what my cholesterol is looking like today. Soon, we shall see. It's a ten minute drive to the lab. There are only two people ahead of me, but still, it takes forty minutes before the vampire has her fill — two vials of blood. Another ten minute drive home and there goes my lunch hour. Oh, well, I wasn't that hungry anyway and, maybe, I can still lose those thirty pounds. Back at home, I log in to work.

Two hours looking at spreadsheets and documents. My one eye begins to water and the telltale flashing lights of the optic migraines to which I am prone begin to appear in my field of vision. I turn off the overhead lights and look away

419

from the computer. I turn my attention to something on paper that will not set off the migraine. Two hours later it is now, six p.m. (or, as they say, *"close enough for government work."*) I log off my computer.

My partner is asking, *"What's for dinner?"* I don't know. I haven't given it any thought. *"Besides,"* I think, *"Wasn't it your turn to make dinner?"* I look in the refrigerator and a single chicken breast is thawed. I guess that I can cook that chicken breast and then add it (along with some vegetables) to ramen noodle soup. *Voilà* – dinner is prepared. (Why am I suddenly reminded of *"The Rocky Horror Picture Show"*? A fleeting memory of my misspent youth passes through my head.)

Dinner is served and we have the usual banal conversation of any married couple. *"How was your day?"* *"Fine, How was yours?"* *"It's your turn to do the dishes."* *"But I did them yesterday!"* As always, a compromise is reached. Ironically, I think, if only politics were as easy as marriage.

I jump in the pool. Twenty more minutes back and forth, back and forth. I step out and see that I am still fat.

I wonder what recorded last night. We still have not watched that last episode of *"Fear the Walking Dead."* We start the recording. In the eyes of the undead, I see my morning self. We continue to watch television as I, sitting with my iPad on my lap, work diligently to revise a couple of chapters of my latest project before bedtime around nine p.m.

Before bed, I use the bathroom and wash my face wondering, where have all the years gone? Then, I look in the mirror and I see those years marching across my face.

Lying in bed, my mind swirls with the events of the day, but I practice my sleep hygiene technique and am snoring away within ten minutes. I pray that I will not have one of my lucid dreams. But, I know that I will. Once that thought comes unbidden to the mind, the fact soon will come to pass.

The next morning, I rise at my usual time — just before six a.m. Like a single-minded zombie (Do zombies have minds?) I stumble from my bedroom to the kitchen (Must have coffee! Must have coffee! Must have coffee!) and turn on the Keurig to warm up. If only these old bones could warm so easily.

JUNE 6, 2018

Unless the chef is in the woods picking berries and hunting wild game, any food you order at a restaurant is *"farm to table."*

Man cannot live on rocks and dirt. All food is organic.

#Sundaytruth

JUNE 17, 2018

I can't be the only one who finds it ironic that:

So many of those who thump their chests in religious fervor, abandon their religious principles in support or opposition to certain government policies. While at the same time . . .

So many of those who proclaim no religious belief, point to religious principles in support or opposition to certain government policies.

This, of course, leads me to consider that perhaps we should *"render unto Caesar that which is Caesar's and unto the Lord that which is His."*

The whole of man is balanced on four pillars:

The soul for spirituality;

The mind for thinking;

The body for physicality; and

The heart for emotions.

But, lately it seems that too many of us don't understand this. Instead,

We have sold our souls.

We have lost our minds.

We use our bodies for love.

We think with our hearts.

Is it any wonder we are unbalanced?

JUNE 20, 2018

I think that I suffer from

palilalia: pali·la·lia (ˌpalə'lālēə/) noun: a speech disorder characterized by involuntary repetition of words, phrases, or sentences.

I think that I suffer from

palilalia: pali·la·lia (ˌpalə'lālēə/) noun: a speech disorder characterized by involuntary repetition of words, phrases, or sentences.

I think that I suffer from

palilalia: pali·la·lia (ˌpalə'lālēə/) noun: a speech disorder characterized by involuntary repetition of words, phrases, or sentences.

These are the things I love about social media:=
Finding someone from your past;
Staying connected to those you thought were left behind;
Sharing thoughts and ideas across the global village.
These are the things I detest about social media:
Finding someone from your past;
Staying connected to those you thought were left behind;
Sharing thoughts and ideas across the global village.

June 22, 2018

I was thinking about writing a book set in a community where most of the grown-ups have disappeared and the children run amok. Then I realized that it had already been written and the community was called "*The Internet.*"

Mario Kiefer

Civility (noun)

Definition   of civility for   English   Language
Learners: polite, reasonable, and respectful behavior.

Definition for modern America: the lost art of . . .

JUNE 24, 2018

When resistance against policy becomes resistance against people, it is not resistance — it is bullying.

JUNE 25, 2018

Life is one long tunnel. If you see a light at the end of the tunnel . . . you are probably dead.

June 30, 2018

When a man goes fishing, he casts a shiny object into the water to lure the fish. When that lure falls in the midst of a school, the fish chase after it, often, fighting each other in their attempts to catch the shiny object. Sometimes, that fighting becomes bloody. The man who cast the line does not care about that. He succeeded in his goal. The fish were distracted and, he feeds on the carcasses.

When the American power structure fishes the seas of the internet, they cast a shiny object into its waters. The object catches the attention of the school of the American public. They fight among themselves in attempt to catch that shiny object; to prove their point or to have their say. All the while not realizing that the object was cast to distract them from the true motivations of the fisherman.

Am I also so distracted?

JULY 1, 2018

I do not pretend to have all of the answers. I know that I
do not. But, at least I am willing to consider another's
thoughts, ideas, arguments and solutions.

Are you?